Fun?

But We're Married!

But We're Married!

A Wise
and
Witty Guide
to a
Lasting Marriage

Lois Leiderman Davitz, Ph.D. & Joel R. Davitz, Ph.D.

SORIN BOOKS   Notre Dame, IN

International Standard Book Number: 1-893732-02-9
Library of Congress Catalog Card Number: 99-61900

Cover design by Cynthia Dunne
Text and interior design by Brian C. Conley
American Gothic by Grant Wood
Friends of the American Art Collection
All rights reserved by the Art Institute of Chicago and VAGA, New York, NY

Printed and bound in the United States of America.

Contents

Introduction

We believe that marriage should be a long, happy honeymoon that only gets better with the passage of time.

And it can be.

We have been married for fifty-four years. For almost that long we have been researching and studying the secrets of a happy marriage—the kind of marriage that is a lasting source of joy. We know it can be done.

And we are here to share with you the secrets we have learned over all those years. We are confident that with them as your guidelines a joyful, lasting marriage can be yours.

Of course, it won't all be easy. There will be ups and downs. We know as well as anyone that a lasting marriage is no snap. It takes more than inertia, a handbook of bedroom techniques, a cold blast of economic pressure, or the threat of family or religious sanctions. You have to turn a lot of stumbling blocks into stepping stones. You have to know how to prevent a crisis from turning into a disaster.

But there is something even more basic.

YOU HAVE TO BELIEVE THAT A LASTING AND HAPPY MARRIAGE IS POSSIBLE FOR YOU AND, MOST IMPORTANTLY, YOU HAVE TO BELIEVE THAT IT IS WORTH THE EFFORT.

Everybody knows that statistics imply that marriages are no longer forever. It's not just that a lot of marriages fail but that the landscape is littered with couples who stay together without, it seems, a shred of happiness in their relationship. We can't dispute such facts. We can't claim that the current odds for a long and happy marriage are all that good. But we can tell you that we are totally and completely certain that this need not be your destiny. Your marriage can last.

Not everybody, of course, agrees that it is worth the effort.

A lot of people can see a long-married couple and, rather than a round of applause, the most they can manage is a quiet "that's nice." For many the idea of living with someone for fifty years is enough to bring on an attack of indigestion. And then there's always someone to wonder aloud: "Why would anyone want to do that?"

Here's why . . .

Marriage—your marriage—can be a source of lasting joy unlike anything else that life offers, an experience of happiness available nowhere else, in no other way. Even in this age of pre-nuptial agreements, marriage is still more than a legal contract, more than a financial agreement, more than mere living arrangements.

By any definition of spirituality that you choose, marriage is the key spiritual experience of most humans, the context in which most of us discover and live out the values that are most important to a full human life: love, fidelity, generosity, and honesty. Marriage lifts us, more than any other experience, beyond our own self-interest.

This is why working for a long-lasting marriage is worth it.

We don't get married to have a spiritual experience—it comes with the territory. We get married because we are in love. We choose not to go through life alone. We want another person in our life with whom we can share our thoughts, dreams, and aspirations—someone with whom we can share not just sorrows but a good laugh.

We want someone to have fun with.

In fact, all those decades ago, and much to the horror of our relatives, we got married to have fun together. ("Don't they know marriage is a serious business?") And we have stayed together because for the most part it's still fun to be with each other.

What more could we wish you?

So have fun together. That's the first piece of advice you'll find in this book . . . but there are other secrets and ground rules that we have discovered over these many years which we hope will help you to be as happy as we have been. Read on.

1
Marriage as Fun

A HAPPY, GLOWING MARRIAGE SHOULD INCLUDE HEALTHY DOSES OF FUN AND SHARED PLEASURE, NOT JUST IN THE HONEYMOON STAGE, NOT JUST AS OCCASIONAL REWARDS AT HOLIDAY TIMES, BUT REGULARLY, EVEN DAILY.

In 1945, marrying at nineteen without a single family member present was a shocking act. In the typical middle-class environments in which we were raised, there were several inviolate laws of male-female relationships which you may find quaintly amusing. The first was that couples did not live together before they were married. Second, couples did not marry without at least grudging approval and family blessings. Such rituals as engagement parties, announcements, the wedding ceremony, and a honeymoon were an absolute must. And last, couples did not marry in their teens, an age considered, then as now, to be a giant step away from maturity. In fact, in any number of states, families could have a marriage annulled on legal grounds if either person was under twenty-one.

Although enormously different in matters of talent, interests, personalities, and abilities, in September, 1945, Joel and I concluded we would never meet another person who would be as interesting, intelligent, beautiful, and dynamic as we imagined each other to be. Given this kind of objective teenage appraisal, marriage made good sense.

Confrontations with a weeping parent or two and a relative who blamed the recent war for pushing people to behave beyond their years, as well as numerous family conferences followed the announcement of our marriage. As you might imagine, these were not happy moments. One cousin came up with the bright suggestion of appealing to Joel's commanding officer: "Isn't that what commanding officers are for? To take care of the men in their charge? He should have Joel court-martialed." (We had been married by a Justice of the Peace at the naval base on St. Simon's Island, Georgia.)

A more rational relative suggested that marriage might not be grounds for court-martial. After all, Joel hadn't been AWOL or anything like that. One formidable aunt, whose wise opinions were held in great respect, analyzed the situation and came up with some predictions which everyone agreed were right on target.

As we reconstructed the story a number of years later, her speech went something like this: "They are foolish, naive children. They have no idea marriage is *serious* business. They have some crazy idea marriage is all fun and games. (Listeners applauded in agreement.) None of the family has to worry. Reality will bring them to their senses. He'll be discharged from the Navy. They'll have no money. They'll come crying to us. No education, no future. They won't be laughing, let me tell you. We don't have to do anything. The marriage will end by itself."

When we returned home to Chicago, one relative, feeling remorse, reluctantly gave a party. Pleased that some peace reigned, we attended, innocently assuming we would be given new tennis rackets (we were avid tennis players then and now), a phonograph player for our 78 RPM collection (the era before CDs), and, above all, new bicycles. One of the problems of the war had been the lack of non essential production. Bicycle manufacturing, as you might expect, had low priority. Our bicycles were battered; mine, a hand-me-down with balloon tires from a brother, and Joel's, an antiquated relic from his twelfth birthday. We hinted broadly about our expected gifts.

In stunned silence, we opened presents. Pots and pans. (For whom? we wondered.) Dish towels. (Was someone making a stupid joke?) A vacuum cleaner with attachments. (Why?) The final blow which threw us into a tailspin of depression was an ironing board and an iron. It was pointed out to us that this was a combination steam and dry iron and more costly than a simple dry heat one.

We did not get married to vacuum, iron, and wipe dishes. Leaving all the presents, we stormed out of the house, bought comforting oatmeal cookies at a corner bakery, and sat on a park bench discussing the depressing afternoon. Our relationship had been built on fun, laughter, and shared pleasure in each other's company. The signals sent by the gifts suggested a vastly different message. Cut out the nonsense. Settle down. Marriage means responsibilities, chores that compound daily, and eventually, if you let them, become unbearable loads. Married life wasn't one long tennis match or bicycle ride; married life was a future sentenced to ironing boards and vacuums.

The implicit message of every gift was deadly seriousness. This, coupled with the lectures about our irresponsibility, pushed us to make a quick decision. We left all the presents behind to be claimed by the givers. Getting into a small car with a few belongings, we headed off to New York where we knew no one, no one knew us and, therefore, no one would care if we chose to experience married life as something to be enjoyed, not just on our honeymoon, but year after year for the fifty years ahead and even longer.

Our adolescent, childish belief that marriage could be one long road of fun and shared pleasure was hardly a novel one. Plenty of young couples believe this on their wedding day. These days, even relatives who feel compelled to warn the happy couple that "marriage isn't easy" will also encourage them to enjoy each other and to always remember why they fell in love. Still, how quickly we forget.

You don't marry or plan to get married to be miserable. You don't marry to nag each other about hair in the bathroom sink, open toothpaste tubes, piles of laundry, bursting hot water heaters, or overdrawn credit cards. On your wedding day you don't whisper to each other or even think to yourself, "How lucky we are to be joined together so someday we can stand in the bedroom, engaged in a shouting match, threatening divorce."

Even though expectations have changed so that pleasure is now an acknowledged goal of married life, many couples still lose sight of the "fun and games" aspect of marriage in an amazingly short time. In one of our studies of married couples, we had them write down all the pleasures they shared with their spouse in the courtship stage. At a later date, we asked the same couples to jot down the activities or pleasures they shared currently. Analysis of the data was shocking. In the early years of the marriage, the lists were long and pretty much identical; however, after a few years, and certainly once the first child was born, there was a precipitous drop of shared fun and pleasure. The lists grew shorter and shorter.

"Of course, life is different," said one of the participants in our study, a young man in his mid thirties. "We have kids now. We're not the same people as we were a few years back."

This young man was right on target. He was 100% correct. A basic fact of life is that people change, and situations change over time. There is no question that at thirty-five this young man wasn't the same person as he had been at twenty-five. He was a husband with kids. But did that mean he and his wife should be through having fun together? He seemed to think so.

We recall one Christmas Eve when a group of graduate students, all struggling on the same inadequate stipends, gathered for a party. Couples exchanged presents. The childless members of our group received frivolous, inexpensive gifts.

The young mother of a six-month-old opened up a rib-boned box, making sure she thriftily saved the paper and the bow. She displayed a buttonholer her husband had bought for the sewing machine. What does one say in any language about a buttonholer for a Christmas present? (For 90s readers, we must explain that sewing was not a hobby then as it more often is now. Bought clothes were more expensive than homemade ones in those days, so most middle-class wives made clothes for themselves and especially for their children.)

That evening has remained etched in our memories. A few years later, when we were doing a pilot study of married couples and marital behavior, we tracked down old friends for cooperation. Unfortunately, this couple, now divorced, could not participate. As another friend from the era explained, "The first wife got a buttonholer; the second, diamond earrings." Obviously, the present's value is not the issue; what is important is what the present says about the meaning and value of the relationship. A buttonholer is practical, work-oriented; earrings, with or without diamonds, are just for fun.

It's so much a part of society's thinking that kids throughout their teens should have fun. They can laugh and play without disapproval. Senior citizens can also indulge themselves. It is assumed they have earned the right to go dancing and to giggle away an evening. In between, well, that's another story. "Settle down; grow up" is the implicit message everyone sends out to glowing, happy honeymooners. And most couples quickly learn how to behave in culturally approved ways. We chose not to.

On our fortieth birthdays (we're a month apart), we bought each other three-speed bicycles with skinny tires instead of the muscle-exhausting, fat balloon tires of the forties. Now any sensible, mature couple with children, owners of a mortgaged, three bedroom, two and one-half bath, split-level house should have known that grass seed and weed killer takes precedence over something as frivolous as bicycles for adults.

Opening the garage doors, we took out our bicycles. A watchful neighbor strolled to the end of his driveway.

"We're all laughing at you," he said. "Heard about the bicycles."

Laughing? Puzzled we examined the shining bicycles. Had we been gypped? Was there something amiss with the design?

"They're great bikes."

"Oh, it's not the bikes, but the idea of adults riding. Pretty funny."

In the middle class, suburban world of the sixties, kids, *not adults*, rode bicycles. A few years after our neighbor and his wife were divorced, we chanced upon him with his new wife on the town bicycle path.

FUN IN A MARRIAGE CAN'T BE TREATED AS A REWARD FOR MOWING LAWNS OR ANY OTHER DUTY PERFORMED

Shaking loose from the idea that ways of behaving and expectations are strictly age-defined is very hard. It's not that the couples in our surveys disagreed with the concept of making sure a spark of fun was still in their marriage, but they saw fun and pleasure as rewards *after* the problems and business of life had been resolved.

The notion of rewarding appropriate behavior is a basic belief of many educators and psychologists. Right behavior must be rewarded. That's how learning occurs. We do this all the time with children. Eat nutritious food and you'll get dessert. Clean up your room and you can watch a video. Perhaps this kind of behavioral reward is appropriate for children, but when transferred to married life it becomes a potential source for disaster.

Six years into their marriage, one couple in our study was flirting with the idea of separation. A house, two children, aged four and six, both with colds, one with chicken pox, a partially flooded basement, a broken screen door, a groaning washing machine, a cleaning service that was unable to get the crayon marks off the new wallpaper in the living room—it all added up to a situation that called for more than a laugh, a kiss, and a quick making-up.

The wife explained, "I had called him several times asking him to come home early. We just couldn't go to the party that night with what was going on in the house. The hot water heater had sprung a leak. Can you imagine trying to heat water on a stove for the kids' baths? It was a nightmare. It just wasn't my day. But you know I've lived with John now for six years. He turns a deaf ear and a closed eye to some of these things. It's all on my back now.

"He just doesn't get it. I mean I'm for fun and games, believe me, but there are priorities. His own mother agrees with me. My mother too. *He's got to grow up.* We're not kids anymore. We have responsibilities. We've got two kids, a house. Anyone in their right mind would know what comes first."

John's side of the story took a different angle. "I knew we couldn't do anything about the heater until the next day. The kids could miss a bath. It wouldn't kill any of us. I felt it was more important to go to that party for an old college friend of mine than to stay at home staring at the broken hot water heater, which is all we could have done anyhow. OK, I didn't go home that evening. She cried all night. Guilting me—sure. But what about me? You know what I saw as my life ahead? One long stretch of broken doors and hot water heaters.

"She's changed. Before we had kids she wouldn't have thought twice about what was right to do. Yes, I did run away. Yes, I still feel like running away. In my mind, I keep thinking, short of a disaster, like lives in danger, when there's something special that's planned, come hell or high water we're going to follow through with our plans."

Whatever your reactions to his behavior, try to imagine how he felt and what he saw staring at him down the years. We knew exactly what he meant. We had our own memories of being chained to a vacuum cleaner with attachments a long time ago.

Pre-married life is based on fun and pleasure. A first date is not followed by a second unless there is the prospect of a second round of fun. We're not necessarily talking about stand-up comedian fun. Pleasure can be dramatically different for each couple. However, no matter the specific circumstances, fun and pleasure are absolute musts if the relationship is going to have a chance to move into the marrying stage. And they are essential if a marriage is going to have a chance to survive.

Unfortunately, it is all too easy to forget to have fun once the honeymoon is over and it is time to go back to work, earn a living, and raise a family. The realities of everyday life, argued one man, take over. Chores of living, the endless minutiae, creep into every facet of daily life and take precedence over fun. In a large-scale study of why couples divorce, without exception, the overwhelming reason for divorce was that the other person was no longer any fun. Although said in a variety of ways, every single individual left their marriage because of no shared interests, no real pleasure. All the spark and magic was gone.

One man said, "She put away the scuba equipment the day after we got back from the honeymoon. I married for fun, and I ended up with an account executive manager." Not every man blames scuba equipment tossed to the back of a closet for casting a pall on the marriage, but each divorced man had a variation on the same theme.

The women in our survey came up with similar complaints. "He watches sitcoms of laughing couples forgetting there's not much to laugh about between the two of us. He brought me flowers and candy when we were dating. Now it's receipts for the dry cleaning he wants me to pick up. Romance after kids? You must be kidding."

The first crisis in marriage is often the *crisis of boredom* with each other. Boredom turns into anger; anger turns into frustration; frustrated, dissatisfied spouses dream of splitting, and, when they dream and plot enough, the split becomes a reality.

Just as couples do not get married so one or the other can nag about unwashed windows, who does the grocery shopping, or who really should care for the kids after a tired day on the job for each of them, no couples ever separate, gripe about each other, or contemplate walking out when they are having fun the way they did in their pre-marriage days.

A MARRIAGE CAN'T AND SHOULDN'T BE RUN
AS IF IT WERE A BUSINESS

All too often when couples hit this kind of wall in their relationships, they assume they can solve the problems with discussion and analysis. It's what one would do in a business. Have conferences; review the issues; study the problems or gripes.

We vividly recall one couple in our study, both young professionals, with one infant, who were ready to call their marriage quits because of the crisis of boredom with each other and resentment of their stereotypical roles. The woman put it this way, "No matter that I have a job, I am expected to do all the maintenance around here, all the house management plus more. I never saw this chauvinistic side to him when we dated. That's for sure."

And, from the young man, "She's the one who's changed. Try to drag her somewhere not on the schedule, and she's armed with excuses. She's got it into her head now that every time I say I won't do something I'm a chauvinist. I have to admit, I have fantasies about freedom. Wouldn't you?"

After extensive marital counseling, thrashing out their anger about boredom, frustration, and the stereotypical roles they were forcing each other to play, they were asked to do some homework. The advisor suggested they jot down everything about their lives that was irritating or that they hated having to do all the time. Writing down one's thoughts can be a very useful therapeutic tool. Written words are a dramatic way of revealing one's thoughts.

The couple compared lists at the next counseling session. Each of the lists fell neatly into stereotypical female and male roles with the exception of changing the kitty litter box, which appeared on both of their lists. Kitty litter boxes do not seem to be as gender typed as vacuuming.

The solution proposed to them was to switch lists, to have a trial period when each of them performed the other's tasks. After a couple of weeks, they met again and divided the lists so each had a good share of their own and the other's chores. This systematic, organized approach, because of its familiar way of dealing with issues, provided the couple with a great deal of comfort. After all, why shouldn't a successful method for business also work in a marriage partnership?

The concept of lists and the exchange of lists made good sense to us, but there was one glaring omission. Nowhere on the lists was mention made of anything that could remotely be considered fun. Life for the couple received high marks for efficiency, but low grades for contentment.

Where were the dates they once had? Where were the few moments of chatting together about something other than broken garbage disposals? Where were the plans for a romantic evening together?

The wife was making sure the car had oil and regular check-ups. The husband took inventory of the kitchen cupboards and made sure they had ample paper towels. But no one was planning candlelight dinners or fun family outings. On a scale of one to ten their score for marital happiness was still a one.

NOTHING SAVES A STUMBLING MARRIAGE MORE THAN RESTORING
FUN INTO THE RELATIONSHIP

Amused and skeptical, they reluctantly experimented with our suggestion that they put some fun in their lives. The first date was a disaster. They felt forced and uncomfortable. "Silly," is how the wife put it. "Pretending we were back in the dating stage, and all that? It was downright embarrassing."

The husband agreed. "Dating is great when you're single," he insisted. He joked about ads in the magazines of people who wanted to meet someone. "Walks in the rain, jogging, music, theater, dancing, Chinese take-out dinners. I'm past that stage," he commented.

They had to be prodded to continue. We reminded them that William James, a 19th century psychologist-philosopher whose ideas remain popular today, believed that if you practice a behavior often and long enough, that behavior will become part of you. It will seem natural. For example, if you practice being good, you will be good. We assured them this would happen with having fun.

Some couples, when they realize their marriage has lost the element of fun, assume that what is lost is gone forever. They feel that making a conscious effort to have fun with someone is somehow false or hypocritical and doesn't "count." It's not easy to have to relearn what you once did so instinctively in your dating stage. It does seem rather odd to have to check calendars and look at appointment books before planning an evening of togetherness. It's not all that easy to remember to stop for flowers on the way home from work. But it is possible, and the fun that you relearn to have may even be more enjoyable than the fun that seemed to come so naturally when you were dating and newly married.

The first breakthrough for this couple came when they were able to laugh at themselves, two awkward adults with a child and a marriage of more than eight years, trying to flirt with each other over a candlelight dinner. But they still had a way to go before they could describe their marriage as fun. One or two fun evenings every month or so is not enough.

FUN—NOT JUST AN EVENING, BUT BUILT INTO
EVERY ASPECT OF YOUR LIVES

Our goal is to have you build the concept of fun, the attitude toward fun into every part of your lives. Fun can get lost after childhood. Of course, as life takes on serious momentum, it's all too easy to forget which should take priority—serious, practical matters or fun.

We vividly recall one time of wavering when we were young faculty members living in a suburban home with monthly payments to meet for car and mortgage. Neighbors in these kinds of "young communities," we soon discovered, were very conscious of each other. There was always a lot of helpful intrusion into others' affairs. For example, if one couple had a driveway resurfaced for appearance's sake, others were encouraged to do likewise.

Construction people, driveway "resurfacers," landscape architects, and crab grass experts worked their way through the community on a regular basis. One spring, a construction company came in persuading everyone to retile their basements and replace walls with lovely panels to create recreation rooms with concealed washers and dryers.

At the same time, the university asked Joel to go to Kampala, Uganda, on a summer research project. This was a wonderful opportunity for adventure. But it would be too expensive for all of us to go—especially if we wanted to keep up with our neighbors' plans for comfortable new basements.

There was a moment of hesitation. Despite the less than wonderful academic salaries, we went off to Uganda.

Construction crews kept knocking on the door. On our return, neighbors showed us spectacular basements. It took us six months of scrimping to pay off airfares for three of us (Joel's fare was paid), and another six months to pay off the debt for all the souvenir spears, drums, masks, and shields the kids collected as we wandered through Africa. The basement was never refinished. In the eighteen years we lived in the house, a coat of gray paint kept cement dust down. Still, we had great stories to tell and memories of some pretty remarkable fun.

The notion of fun, an attitude toward our life together that we dedicated ourselves to at age nineteen and worked to keep in mind over the passing years, has not been an accident or a matter of chance. Keeping the spark of fun alive and flourishing in your marriage won't always be easy. There are going to be inevitable down times.

Yes, it may be a naive attitude. Perhaps our awareness of our determination to have fun takes on special importance as we grow older. We realize it isn't easy when you are in the developing stages of a marriage to keep in mind the importance of filling every minute with a full measure of sixty happy seconds. Age gives one this kind of wisdom. It's an insight that underscores our half century plus of marriage. "They think marriage is fun and games," warned the doom and gloomers. A half century ago, when we sat on a park bench munching oatmeal cookies thinking about unending years of fun and shared pleasure, we were the wise ones.

2 Rules of Battle

Like death and taxes, marital fights are inevitable—and about as pleasant. The frequency, duration, and intensity will, of course, vary from couple to couple. However, an indisputable fact of life is that some form of quarreling goes hand-in-hand with marriage.

If you have difficulty accepting this concept, we assure you we felt the same way. The idea that we would ever fight was inconceivable. Parents argued; relatives quarreled; other couples fought—not us. We were above all that childish nonsense. While it is true that in our pre-marriage courtship stage we had a few spats, none of them ever reached great, dramatic proportions. They were merely minor disagreements, usually over such insignificant matters as where to have dinner or what film to see.

LOVER'S QUARRELS—A NECESSARY FIRST
INTRODUCTION TO MARRIAGE

We had only one difference that seemed to us to be really earthshaking. Looking back, it definitely fit the category of a lover's quarrel. We're convinced these kinds of disputes are pretty much a rite of passage, necessary for individuals to assure each other of the strength of their love and commitment before taking the final step to the altar.

Our serious pre-marriage argument was about valentines, specifically the one I didn't get on Valentine's Day. But then it arrived—merely late. It had the traditional paper lace cutouts, oversized hearts, and a carefully composed message by an employee from the Hallmark corporation expressing Joel's undying love and fidelity. My anger and disappointment dissipated. I was pacified, and happily pasted it in a scrapbook.

Other than this one lapse, our disagreements were very much on the light side. Wounded feelings were readily soothed. Our differences were small radar blips on the screen and they soon disappeared.

What really mystifies us is how an official marriage ceremony, a license, and pastoral blessings dramatically change the status quo. Once married, couples, including ourselves, can justifiably and officially fight. They're tied together. Their futures will be littered with occasional or even frequent disagreements.

None of this is planned. When the fights start to happen, everyone appears so surprised, even shocked. Suddenly couples feel mature. Innocence in the relationship is gone. There's no going back to the carefree days where never or seldom was a harsh or unpleasant word spoken, never a moment when one or the other wanted "out." Reality of married life settles in to stay.

FIGHTING IS CULTURALLY CONDITIONED

Before we go into this matter in more depth, explaining and illustrating how fighting need not destroy your relationship or seriously threaten your togetherness, and may, in fact, be productive, we do think it interesting to point out that not all cultures engage in the marital sport of arguing or fighting.

Two of our Hopi friends, for over forty years, never had any verbal combat or said unpleasant, cross words to each other. We assumed, from the outside, that their marriage was tranquil, peace loving, and strong. How marvelous. It was just the way other people saw our marriage—from the outside. Easygoing, relaxed, and *totally free from conflict.*

You can imagine our shock on a recent visit to their village on one of the Hopi mesas in Arizona to discover that they had separated. Obviously there had been long-standing, unresolved grievances which were never made verbally explicit but which were fully understood by the parties involved. The husband packed his suitcase and moved down the dusty rocky road, a distance of 1/3 of a mile. The wife remained in the original adobe home.

Every day at noon, he ambles down the path for lunch with his wife. After lunch, he hooks up his TV to the car, mounted on cinder blocks, and spends a couple of hours watching favorite TV programs. (She kept the television set. Since the mesa does not have electricity, he has a complex system arranged which involves using the car alternator and battery to provide power.) Their routine is unfailing. Respectful, considerate, polite as always, they have a very nice, easy, mainly nonverbal relationship. Hopis are not given to long dialogues or monologues and would consider the typical loud and hostile verbal arguments of our culture most unseemly.

Another friend of ours is an American with a native-born Japanese wife. Like the Hopis, Japanese people deplore verbal confrontation. In fact, they will go to inordinate lengths to avoid such encounters. This couple, married for well over three decades, has one major problem.

"She won't fight. It drives me crazy. I lose my temper and all she does is sit down at the table and look at me."

He soon finds himself role-playing, taking his point of view, making up her side of the story, in effect arguing with himself. He soon finds that keeping up this monologue at a rapid, high-pitched pace is not only rather unpleasant but makes him feel downright foolish.

For the past twenty-five years, in cooperation with Japanese colleagues, we have conducted many studies concerned with Japanese and American cultures. One of these research studies involved a comparison of Japanese and American marriage and divorce. Since we had discussed the study with this friend, there was no problem asking her questions.

"Do you ever provoke a fight?"

"Never."

"When your husband initiates an argument, what do you do? Do you argue back or . . . ?"

"Nothing." (She seemed astonished that we expected her to *do something*.)

"What are your expectations regarding his behavior?"

"He'll calm down after all that excited chatter."

"Does he?"

"Of course." It was clear from her tone that, if he were so foolish as to carry on like that, she certainly wouldn't encourage such nonsense. It was not the Japanese way—such displays of temper are considered childish.

"Think back to the last time you had an argument. When was that?"

"Yesterday."

"All right, tell us what happened?"

"He was angry about something. I really can't recall. The harangue started at 1 p.m. exactly. At 2:15 he was still carrying on."

"Where were you?"

"Sitting at the kitchen table consulting cookbooks."

"While he was raising his voice and arguing, what went through your mind? Please be specific."

(We fully expected a whole range of murderous fantasies. Her reply was totally unexpected.)

"Basmati rice."

"Basmati rice!"

"Of course Basmati. It couldn't be Jasmine. We were having guests for dinner. I was going to make Indian curry. I ran out of Basmati rice."

So much for marital fighting among the Japanese and Hopis. Such stoic silence or minimal verbal exchange is unthinkable for those of us raised in the western world. We are taught to voice our disagreements, to get them out in the open. We quickly learn to stand up for ourselves, to argue for our own point of view, sometimes quite loudly.

In fact, we realize, if there weren't marital disputes, a great deal of what passes for American literature, movies, television dramas, theater, soap operas—a whole world of entertainment— would simply disappear. Marital fighting is a recognized, expected activity when American writers think of portraying marriage. This makes theatrical sense. It's hard to imagine maintaining much interest in a dramatic play consisting of a husband and wife paying each other compliments and sending love messages. The thought of such dullness is numbing.

It is beyond the scope of this book to analyze why exactly the implicit message of the marriage license is the approval of arguments or fights. It isn't as if the two people involved have been stalking each other, impatiently waiting for the ceremony, so they can explode with repressed hostility. The delayed valentine was the only real upset we had that led to harsh words before marriage. However, it didn't take us very long for us to conform to cultural expectations. And the remarkable fact is we didn't need any practice or training in what to say, how to express our thoughts, how to blame, accuse, transfer guilt. Everything was quite intuitive.

Our first bitter words occurred at the end of a four-day honeymoon. Joel's naval air station was on St. Simon's Island. We were married in Brunswick, Georgia, a town across the causeway from the Navy air base. The day after the ten minute ceremony Joel had a long weekend pass, and we decided to honeymoon in Savannah, Georgia.

Hopping a bus (we didn't have a car), we had a perfect few days in Savannah, a city famous for its magnolia trees, lovely residential areas, and restaurants. Balmy September weather and the end of the war in the Orient combined to make ours a truly romantic adventure.

Reluctantly, we packed our duffel bag for the return bus trip to St. Simon's. That's when Joel discovered our one problem. We had no money.

"You mean we don't have any money left for bus tickets?"

Joel nodded his head in affirmation.

"For breakfast?"

"No money for breakfast either."

"How could you let this happen?"

"Are you blaming me? That's nuts. What about you? You should have thought, too. Remember we're in *this* together." ("This" referred to the marriage.)

We scrounged through every single pocket but found nothing. Now remember, this was September 10, 1945. Living from paycheck to paycheck, we did not have a bank account. And, even if we had had a bank account with money, there wasn't anything like ATMs for quick withdrawals. We didn't know anyone in Savannah. The pawn shops wouldn't be open until noon, and we didn't really have much to pawn except perhaps our new wedding rings which cost twenty dollars apiece. That idea did cross our minds, but even as our tempers flared, it seemed like it would be going a bit too far to pawn our rings four days into the marriage.

After a few moments of stunned silence, we were ready to engage in full battle. Accusations flew back and forth as we took turns accusing each other of forgetfulness, lack of planning, overspending on dinner and the purchase of a couple of typical souvenirs, including his and hers towels with printed pictures of Bull Street, Savannah's famous historic main boulevard.

"OK, I'll take the towels back. We won't have a thing to remember from our honeymoon. If that will make you happy, that's exactly what I'll do." (Said with a great deal of sarcasm.)

"I hate those towels. I thought they were stupid when you bought them."

"Why didn't you say anything? You lied to me. You said you liked them. It's what I can expect. I chose them so naturally you think they're dumb."

We honestly had no idea what we were going to do. Joel had to be back at the base. Our only alternative was to try to hitchhike, an idea we both came up with at the same time. Hitchhiking before and during the war was *not* considered dangerous. Perhaps it was the heritage of the Depression era when getting around by means of thumbing rides was very common. Everyone did it at one time or another. Actually, we had no other choice. It didn't occur to us to go to the police or the hotel manager mostly, I suppose, because of embarrassment. Besides, it was highly unlikely that the manager would have believed us; he would almost certainly have assumed it was some con game.

I changed from jeans to my flowered cotton wedding dress and put on tennis shoes for the long walk. Joel put on his blue-gray Navy officer's uniform and his Navy hat. We must note that Navy uniforms were and still are quite dashing. Our idea was that, dressed appropriately, we might tempt some driver to stop.

We hiked out to the edge of town and stared at the long stretch of cracked macadam that led off into the flat horizon. In '45, the outskirts of Savannah were *deserted*. The sun was coming up. Hungry and tired, I sat down on a rock, and we argued some more, our words a little more high pitched, tinged with more bitterness and blame.

A miserable hour passed without a car. Remember this was '45. In this part of Georgia there weren't too many people with cars. There wasn't even a house as far as we could see.

"Do you have money back at the base?" Now I was just getting curious; money at the base could not possibly help us in our predicament. Something was amiss with my logic, but logic rarely concerns two combatants.

"No."

"How did we take this honeymoon?"

"I borrowed money from Eddie. I figured he's taken enough from me at poker games. You know, I think that guy was born with a deck of cards in his hand."

"You know he's a card shark. He cheats. I'm sure of it."

Now we started bickering about this officer who was a card shark, the unofficial banker for the innocent young officers who felt Eddie was ripping them off but couldn't prove anything. We began to squabble about this guy. You can imagine the absurdity. We are sitting on a dusty highway early in the morning, hungry, with no money and no transportation, and we're fighting about this guy who may or may not cheat at cards. (Before you judge our behavior too harshly, please review some of your own recent arguments.)

Anyhow, our displaced rage with Eddie did nothing to bring St. Simon's any closer, but for a few moments, we did feel somewhat less tense. I discovered a package of orange Lifesavers in my handbag. (Keep these Lifesavers in mind. They play an important role in our next conflict.) Now, even though we were most unhappy with each other, I did share the Lifesavers. Just as we were feeling very desperate one of those chance occurrences happened that can make one believe in miracles.

A car materialized at breakneck speed. We jumped up and down waving madly. The car passed, screeched to a halt, and backed up.

"What the hell are you two doing here?" It was Joel's commanding officer, returning from a weekend in Savannah, driving a smashing convertible.

Puzzled, he twisted around looking out at the stark landscape. "Your car break down?" It took him a few minutes to realize that we didn't have a car. The rusted vehicle lying on its side behind the barbed wire fence could hardly have been ours.

"Hop in." He took us back to the base. Joel did his best to make appropriate Navy small talk. I pouted in the back seat.

When we reached the Navy base, after thanking him for saving us from a long walk, I asked, "When is payday?"

"Friday," was his response. "Going to make it?"

Later that day, still smarting from the morning's outbursts, we went to the elegant country club pool not far from the base on a nearby island. In return for permitting officers and their families to use the exclusive facilities, a renowned Sea Island luxury spa hotel avoided having the Navy commandeer rooms for Navy personnel.

I climbed to the top of the high dive. Although I had my lifesaving badges, I was not a great diver. However, aware that Joel was watching, I deliberately dove off the high dive.

"You could have broken your neck," my husband of four days told me.

"That would have made you happy," I replied. "You'd be free at last."

"Well, not exactly. I couldn't afford the funeral. Not until Friday."

Being newly-weds, it didn't take us long to recover from this first fight. We considered it, perhaps, a momentary aberration.

Surely we didn't expect a repeat performance before the week was out. But that was just what we got.

And somehow, in just two fights, we managed to break just about every rule that in our later and wiser years we realized were essential to preserving a happy marriage despite inevitable conflicts.

First, let us share with you the Orange Lifesaver War and then we'll look at the rules of battle that Joel and I have worked out since we negotiated these early battlefields.

OUR SECOND MAJOR CONFLICT

Our first home, in the period before I returned to the University of Michigan for my senior year and Joel finished his final ten months in the Navy, was a large room in someone's home on St. Simon's Island. The owner of the residence, a widow, had four spare bedrooms, and she rented each of them to a Navy couple. A generous Southern lady, she assigned each of us one shelf in her refrigerator for our personal supply of food, warning us to mark everything clearly. We also had specific times when we could use two burners of the stove.

Since there were few restaurants in the area, and families could not eat on the base, some cooking was necessary. The limitations of shelf space posed somewhat of a burden. In addition, it was also a long walk to the town grocery. Doing a lot of grocery shopping was difficult.

However, one day we lucked out. The wife of the ensign who lived in the adjoining room knocked on our door and told us we could have her shelf in the refrigerator because she was returning home to her parents. Her husband, a regular Navy officer, was being assigned overseas for an indeterminate tour of duty.

The good news was exciting. When Joel returned home from flight duty, we marched off to town. With visions of that extra shelf in mind, we did a major shopping, and, by the time we were ready to return home, we had two huge paper sacks of groceries. My final purchase at the check-out counter was two packages of orange Lifesavers.

I must explain the orange Lifesavers in more detail. On first reading you will probably dismiss them with a "so what" flippancy. Unless you are an addict of some sort, you cannot appreciate the importance of those orange Lifesavers. I always had a supply in my pocket or handbag. Running out of Lifesavers could cause serious withdrawal symptoms. I was definitely emotionally dependent.

We started back, choosing to take a short cut along the old road that paralleled a swamp. It was hot. We were hungry and tired. About halfway back Joel stopped.

"Why the hell did you buy all this c . . . . ?"

"Food," I retorted. "Remember, we have to eat."

"I think this is crazy."

"What's so crazy about eating? You like to eat a helluva lot more than me."

"Says who?"

"I said that."

"Do you realize what I look like?"

"You look like someone carrying groceries," I commented.

"Do you have any idea who I am? No, of course not. You think only of yourself. You are totally egocentric."

"I know who you are."

"OK, who am I?"

"You are Joel carrying groceries."

"No g . . .d . . . it. I am a naval officer and naval officers *do not* carry groceries."

"Oh, so that's what they write in those manuals you're reading. What a huge governmental waste of money. Joel shouldn't carry groceries. Rule one. Your poor macho image will be all screwed up." And, of course, I "singsonged" my retort.

Joel's feet became rooted to the ground. He put down the bags, took out my orange Lifesavers, both packs, and *flung* them into the swamp. (As I write these words today, I can still feel a visceral reaction to the gesture.)

At the time I was speechless. Although the craving was great, I would not give him the satisfaction of searching for the packages. Inside I was shaking. It was the worst sort of humiliation that I could have possibly imagined. If feminism had been active, I would have marched in Washington. It was a distinctive male act of female domination.

"I am leaving you tomorrow," was all I could say.

"Go ahead," was Joel's immediate response.

We stopped speaking the rest of the way back. I made a sandwich for myself and sat out on the roof eating. One window in our room opened up to the roof, and we could crawl out and sit on the gable when the weather wasn't too hot. Joel joined me. I turned my back. This was a major quarrel.

The hurt was so great that we thought it best not to discuss the matter. The next day, Joel brought me six packages of orange Lifesavers from the "ship store." He still didn't get it. It wasn't the replacement of the Lifesavers that mattered but his deliberately hostile act of throwing the original two rolls away. Lest you think we totally forgot or repressed this event, we should tell you about our 45th anniversary sentimental return to St. Simon's Island.

After cycling during the afternoon on the hard sandy beaches, we rode over to one area, wondering if "they" were still there. Without saying anything, we both knew we were looking for orange Lifesavers.

THE RULES OF FIGHTING SAFELY AND PRODUCTIVELY

In a perfect world, couples would intelligently settle their differences with rational verbal behavior. "We haven't money for bus tickets," said at the end of a honeymoon might be answered with a comment such as, "How unfortunate. We must think of some solution to our dilemma."

A male *or* female, accused of philandering, might say, "Yes, dear, I have been indiscreet. My errant behavior will not be repeated. I think compassion and forgiveness are in order."

"Of course, dear, I totally understand," would be the calm response.

There would be no need for dishes flying, doors banging, language one didn't even dream one knew being shouted. However, sadly enough, this is not a perfect world. That simply isn't how most couples interact.

It's not too difficult to understand the pervasiveness of some degree of conflict in most American marriages. After all, in the intimate day-to-day interactions of a married couple, there are countless opportunities for disagreement ranging from the choice of favorite toothpaste to major decisions about child-rearing. Just by chance, any two people faced with the innumerable possibilities of conflict are bound to have some discord. And it is these disagreements which are the kernels of marital fights.

We have studied a number of American couples who have gone to extraordinary lengths to avoid fighting. By and large we regret to report that this strategy doesn't seem to be very effective. All too often the suppression of overt conflict results in smoldering tension that eventually erupts with drastic consequences. In Japan, the general strategy of *suppressing overt conflict* is buttressed and reinforced by a long tradition of cultural values, and, thus, conflict suppression works for the Japanese. But, in the United States, we don't have the cultural values and mechanisms that support the suppression of overt conflict; therefore, rather than suffer the underlying tension and discomfort of inhibited conflict, it seems much more useful for American couples to face their disagreements and deal with them openly even at the risk of fighting.

But, it is also true that fighting can be very painful and may seriously hurt the relationship. *Our goal, therefore, is to provide you with intelligent, rational, and above all, useful insights which will enable to you to fight safely, productively, without leaving any residue of ill will.* Most important of all, we will discuss how to learn from a fight, a lesson which, in the long run, could be of immeasurable help in reducing stress and tension when a new disagreement occurs.

THE RULE OF CONSISTENCY

First of all it is important to recognize that every couple develops a *unique and consistent pattern of fighting.* In our own personal experience, we have been astonished by the remarkable consistencies of our behavior over half a century. More than fifty years ago, when we were arguing about orange Lifesavers, Joel took the role of prosecutor and Lois, defense attorney, roles that we still play in our current squabbles. And, in our most recent conflicts about money, Joel's cavalier attitude towards money is in sharp contrast to my own conservative and more thoughtful stance, which are the same positions we took during our honeymoon. However, no matter the content, or your patterns, the insights we have developed cut across differences among couples.

THE RULE OF SPECIFICITY

Keep your disagreements focused on the immediate issue at hand. One couple we interviewed noted that every time they disagreed, whether it was about children, money, or where to go on a vacation, the husband ended up talking about how difficult he found his mother-in-law and the wife wound up accusing him of being selfish and controlling. As a result, their arguments rarely resolved the specific issues that initiated the conflict, and their fights often escalated into major emotional storms.

The danger of generalizing in a marital conflict is that the fighting easily gets out of control. A couple begins with a relatively simple issue such as which television program to watch, but quickly broadens the discussion to cover personality traits. As a result, the goal of selecting a television program is hopelessly lost. Sometimes this can reach outlandish proportions such as on our honeymoon, when we argued about Eddie, the poker player, and whether he cheated at cards, when the real issue was how we were going to get home.

Not only should couples avoid generalizing over topics, they should also avoid generalizing over time. Any sentence that begins "You always . . ." or "You never . . ." should be a red flag that this kind of generalizing is going on. No one always forgets to put their shoes away or never remembers to call when they'll be home later than planned. Bringing up past examples doesn't help to deal with the current problem. When arguments get lost in history, resolution of current conflicts becomes virtually impossible. In the throes of an argument, we sometimes find ourselves going over something that happened anywhere from ten to fifty plus years ago. Orange Lifesavers die hard.

THE RULE OF ROLES

A well-established fact in the study of animal behavior is that in many intra-species conflicts each animal takes a more or less consistent role. A dominant wolf, for example, bears his fangs in an act of aggression, and a less dominant wolf reacts by clearly submissive behavior. The role of each wolf in the conflict remains remarkably consistent over time. Very much the same thing is true in human marital conflicts. A very common pattern involves one spouse playing the role of prosecuting attorney and the other the role of defense lawyer.

"Why was all that money spent on something we'll never use?" says one spouse about the purchase of an expensive leaf roto blower.

"I thought we could use it."

"We only have two trees! Last year you did the same thing. You bought a chain saw, and you sawed one log."

"That's not true. I used it more than once."

"No, just once. What else did you saw?"

"I don't remember, now!"

And so the argument goes, with the "prosecutor" trying to build a case, and the "defense lawyer" trying to establish reasonable doubt. The problem with this sort of role-playing is that the pseudo legal conflict takes on a life of its own, generating its own momentum. The main thrust of the prosecutor's efforts is to prove that his or her spouse is guilty of some marital crime, while all the efforts of the defending spouse are aimed at countering the prosecutor's attacks and escaping from guilt. Lost in this marital legal battle of attack and defense is the initial problem that sparked the conflict, and also lost, of course, is any hope of dealing with the problem in a potentially productive way.

This happened during the preparation of this manuscript. Joel had some notes prepared which he gave me. I was redoing a section on the computer and incorporated his notes with all the changes. I cleaned up the desk as I do at stages and everything was dumped into the trash.

Joel wanted to revise the section. "Where are the notes?"

"I used them. I cleaned up."

"You threw my notes away?"

"Not exactly. I used them first."

"Why did you throw them away?"

"I didn't exactly throw them . . . "

"No, they crumpled themselves up and walked to the garbage."

"You didn't tell me you wanted to keep them!"

"Why should I have to tell you not to throw away *my* notes?"

The next thing I knew I was frantically going through the garbage, realizing the notes went down the trash chute a long time ago. My defense was crumbling. His prosecution stepped up. The old familiar roles were in high gear.

While prosecution and defense are the roles Joel and I are most likely to assume during an argument, other couples may choose other roles. One may be prone to playing the martyr in every altercation, making the other the "bad guy" every time. Or perhaps one tries to play the savior, rescuing their spouse from his or her own flaws. Think about your own conflicts. What roles do you and your spouse consistently play?

With all these roles, the danger is that the role-playing will take on a life of its own and distract from the real issue of the argument. Then the argument becomes more about laying blame or avoiding guilt than anything else. The "prosecution" only rests when the "defense" pleads guilty. The "martyr" may give in but only if the other is willing to accept being the "bad guy" yet again. The "savior" may come up with a solution but only if the "helpless" one can stomach being rescued.

Remember that in marital fights, rarely, if ever, is one person entirely at fault and the other completely blameless. If you dig deep enough into almost any conflict between two people, both of them have contributed to their disturbed interaction. And be especially careful of falling into your favorite roles, roles that you may play with relish, but which, in the long run, are likely to make your marital fights much worse than they need be.

All of us have especially sensitive areas that must definitely be off-limits in a marital fight. In boxing there is a well-known rule: Don't hit below the belt. Even though two boxers may be moving in for the kill, determined to flatten each other in the ring, by and large, they refrain from hitting below the belt. Married couples should take heed. No matter how bad the fight is, stay away from off-limit topics that will only serve to enrage or devastate your spouse.

As one woman said, "He can attack me, yell, rant about everything, but when he gets on to some argument with me he better not bring up my putting on a few pounds or I swear I'll have his head on a platter."

Strong words certainly. Her wise husband knew this. On the other hand, she knew that in the course of a spat she had better not mention even one word about his losing that gorgeous shock of hair he once had.

In our own relationship, no matter the original topic under heated discussion I would never dream of calling Joel a "bad father to our sons." This would be hitting way below the belt. By the same token, he would never dare to accuse me of being wasteful with money. We both know full well I am more concerned about money than he is and attacks like that are far too dangerous to even think about.

On the other hand, just as everyone has sensitive areas that are forbidden topics of fighting, every couple also has safe topics that they can comfortably quarrel about year after year. After more than five decades, we blink in astonishment at the number of times we have been at each other about my cooking. Of course, a current argument may not start with cooking but somehow we frequently end up on that topic. It's a safe and well-practiced way for Joel to fight. And no matter what initiates a conflict, I usually shift to my own preferred topic of fighting, Joel's assumed perfection and dogmatism. "You're not so perfect. You're dogmatic. You have no right to play professor in this house."

On it goes, Joel proclaiming me a lousy and thoughtless cook and my exclaiming about his lack of perception and professorial dogmatism. For us, these are safe and comfortable topics for fighting with well-rehearsed speeches that each of us has made dozens of times. Above all we avoid those forbidden, sensitive topics that are "below the belt" for each of us.

THE RULE OF TIME AND PLACE

Marital fighting is a very personal matter. We remember with a great deal of discomfort the first time friends of ours fought in our presence. The fact that they were fighting at all was surprising since we had naively assumed they were gloriously at ease with each other twenty-four hours a day and not at all like us lesser mortals. They "lost it" publicly at a dinner party, no less, and we, and the other guests, cringed, raising the level of our speech to drown out the angry words, not daring to look at the couple or even at each other.

Children can fight publicly. Strangers can get into words about almost anything, even something as trivial as a parking space, but for married couples to engage in disputes in the presence of others is clearly to be avoided. Fighting in public simply increases ten-fold the attendant shame, guilt, tension, and embarrassment associated with a marital fight. It makes the interpersonal situation between husband and wife infinitely more complex, and makes any hope of reasonable resolution much more remote than it needs to be. Therefore, keep your fights private. Remember that old, but useful, cliché, "Don't air your dirty laundry in public."

Just as there is a proper place for fighting, there is also a proper time for marital fights. The general rule to follow is don't hit the other person when he or she is down. When your spouse is sick or overly tired or very worried about something, and you feel bouncy, energetic, worry free, and raring to go, you must do whatever you can to avoid fighting. It just isn't fair; while you may score a quick knockdown early in the fight, you're also likely to feel guilty, and your spouse unjustly and unfairly put upon. *Not all is fair in love and war.* Even in war there are Geneva conventions that prohibit certain behaviors. In marital fighting, we can be at least as civilized by remembering to fight fairly in a proper place and at the proper time.

THE RULE OF CONTROLLED ANGER

One of the problems with fighting is that anger tends to escalate. The initial conflict that triggers a fight may have generated only some mild irritation, but as the process of fighting ensues, this irritation may gradually build into a major storm of anger.

Part of this kind of emotional escalation derives from the experience of being attacked in the course of a fight. No one enjoys being attacked, and a normal reaction is to become increasingly angry. Thus, the dynamics of the fighting process itself carry with them the seeds of escalation. A number of the rules we have proposed such as *the rule of specificity, the rule of forbidden topics,* and *the rule of time and place* are aimed at modifying the fighting process with the goal of reducing the rate at which anger escalates.

However, there is another, perhaps even more subtle source of this emotional escalation. This source is the fighter's own behavior. There is a self-generating quality of behavior that expresses anger. As you hear yourself angrily yelling or sense yourself angrily pounding the table, you become even angrier. The anger *breeds* on itself through your awareness of your own behavior. Your angry behavior also serves to elevate the response of your spouse.

We therefore propose that you consciously curb your behavior in order to minimize the self-generating aspect of angry fighting. It should be abundantly clear by this point that we are *not* recommending a strict and stoic emotional inhibition that would hardly be congruent with our own personal styles. However, some conscious control of the expression of anger can serve the very important purpose of making the fighting a good deal safer.

USING THE RULES

If you follow the rules of marital fighting, we guarantee that your fights will be less hurtful, more reasonably controlled, and much less likely to leave you scarred from highly charged emotional conflicts that have gotten out of hand. However, from time to time in the heat of the battle, despite our best intentions, we have found ourselves breaking the rules. After all these years of self-study as well as research into the behavior of other married couples, Joel occasionally slips into the role of prosecuting attorney, and I sometimes tread on one of Joel's very sensitive, "forbidden" areas. You will likely do the same from time to time. That's O.K.

Even if you don't follow the rules 100% of the time, simply knowing the rules can be very useful. There have been many times when Joel has begun building a case proving my guilt, and I feel somewhat overwhelmed because I haven't prepared my defense properly. The reminder that he is playing prosecuting attorney again can serve as a check to his behavior. In the incident of the lost notes, after we had gone through a bit of a scene, we reminded each other that his prosecuting attorney stance and my hitting below the belt were really being non productive. The edge was taken off the attack and this curbed any further hurtful, fighting behaviors.

When couples first begin fighting, for the most part they do not understand or even see the dynamics. They fight blindly, throwing a lot of hits and punches that go nowhere. With some understanding of the process, one can take a more matter-of-fact approach, reminding the other person of the role he or she is assuming. Most importantly, knowing the rules offers some sense of control so the fight doesn't go wildly on in all directions leaving both spouses bewildered, not knowing how to pick up the pieces of their lives to go forward.

THE POST-FIGHT HUDDLE

Even in the happiest and most successful of marriages, there are bound to be some aspects of the relationship that fall short of perfection. Given the enormous complexity of human interactions, the stresses and demands every couple encounters, the pace of our lives, and the powerful forces operating in our environments, it is little wonder that few, if any of us, reach an ideal state of total marital bliss.

Thus, marital relationships, like every other ongoing human relationship, need some adjustments from time to time. Sometimes, the necessary adjustments are minor, like agreeing to buy separate toothpastes for each spouse. Once in a while, more important and significant adjustments are required. After all, marriage is a dynamic relationship that inevitably involves some changes over time.

The important point to note is that the feedback information about your marriage, the information that is crucial in making the necessary adjustments in your marital relationship, often comes from marital fights. It is precisely in those moments of conflict and discord that husband and wife communicate to each other critical information about what kinds of adjustments need to be made in their relationship. Marital fighting, therefore, can serve a most important function by providing an opportunity for a husband and wife to get the feedback they need to make adjustments in their day-to-day living with each other. Marital fighting, when conducted safely, can help couples achieve a happier and even more successful relationship.

But this kind of listening to each other and learning from your listening is not likely to occur most effectively in the throes of a fight. Usually, we are too caught up in the emotional *sturm and drang* of the fight to listen to each other with care, much less to learn from this listening.

That's why we have devised the "post-fight huddle." Sometimes we "huddle" an hour after the fight, sometimes a day or two later. We wait until our emotions have calmed down, but not so long that we will forget what was communicated during the fight. Then, we ask ourselves what each of us was trying to communicate during the fight.

Of course, a lot of the communication that goes on during the fight is emotional noise, and we have to be careful with each other to recognize the noise as noise and not start the bickering again. But when we manage to filter this emotional noise, more often than not, we get a kernel of information that triggers the adjustment process, the process that is so important in achieving a happy marriage. We learn something about each other's disappointments, frustrations, irritations, and discomforts, and we get a chance to help each other and ourselves.

The post-fight huddle isn't easy, and success doesn't come automatically. We had to work at it for a long time, often running the emotional risk of starting up a fight again. But eventually we learned to listen to each other, to separate the useful information from the angry noise, and to use this information in making our relationship a good deal happier than it was the day Joel threw those orange Lifesavers into the swamp.

Sometimes in the course of our marital fighting we find ourselves going round and round in increasingly vicious circles. The original problem that started the conflict is long forgotten. The dynamics of the fighting process itself take over, and we are caught in a hopeless muddle of escalating hostility.

It was during one of those times of senseless fighting that we made one of the most important discoveries of our married life: FAST FORWARD.

We're not certain which one of us first started using the phrase, but we both knew immediately what it meant. STOP ATTACKING. STOP DEFENDING. STOP EVEN TRYING TO ARGUE. In short, simply stop fighting. It may come when you're in the middle of what you believe to be a devastating attack or a brilliant defensive move. It may come at a moment of irrational yelling or tears or table pounding. But the rule is: Just stop it and move your life on fast forward.

The example we gave of our argument about the notes threatened progress. Our words reached a crescendo. I was accused of doing the same thing with some notes thirty-five years ago. I countered that those notes were on a different topic anyhow and were certainly useless now. We were breaking every rule in this chapter and any move forward was blocked. Just as we were moving in for killer attacks about trust in each other, one of us gained enough control to cry out the famous "fighter's" surrender: FAST FORWARD!

When we first started using the term, the magic of fast forward as a way of altering our behavior was difficult for us to accept. In our professional lives we were used to dealing with problems rationally, reasoning our way through the complexities of a psychological research study until we reached a solution. But this type of rational problem solving didn't always work well in our personal lives, especially when we were in conflict with each other. Sometimes, the best thing we could do was simply drop the discussion, stop the fighting, and muddle our way through our daily lives without coming to any explicit, rational decision.

The magic of fast forward lies in the fact that, more often than not, this muddling works. The case of the lost notes illustrates this beautifully. Desperate, we resorted to our fast forward technique. Tempers calmed down. I could stop looking through the wastebasket and drawers for something I knew wasn't there to begin with. Joel could stop bringing up the other times when his notes somehow were buried under books or papers. Instead of being locked into a dead-end future, we were able to think of the obvious solution which was to reconstruct ideas we had discussed from the rough drafts still in our possession.

The fast forward technique won't always help you work out a problem. Every once in a while you just will have to live with an unresolved problem that defies a rational solution. In any event, when you find yourselves going around in nasty, vicious circles, when you seem to be fighting largely for the sake of fighting, when a rational solution seems hopelessly out of reach, we urge you to try our favorite invention: FAST FORWARD.

3
When Less Is More

In the middle-class 40s world in which we grew up, families, friends, and acquaintances didn't analyze every word or think much about the psychological implications of what they said to each other. It's not that people went out of their way to be rude or hurtful, but no one we knew obsessed or even thought very much about what they said. In fact, we seriously doubt that ordinary people, like our friends and families, ever imagined that communication between husband and wife or families was any big deal. People just talked. In-depth analysis of the meaning and implications of the consequences of the communication process was hardly of concern.

For example, when Aunt Else, well into middle age and overly excited at her daughter's wedding, forgetting she had had far too many refills of champagne, pranced out onto the dance floor to do a solo rumba, her eighty-five-year-old mother had no guilt feelings when she said, "Trust my daughter Else to make a fool of herself. She finally gets her daughter married and this is what she does."

Was this grandmother chastised for her public indiscretion? Absolutely not. Did anyone worry about Aunt Else's psyche? Hardly. Did anyone imagine Aunt Else would feel the rejection of her mother and never speak to her again? Unthinkable. Else knew, as did everyone else, that Grandma was a wise, intelligent, perceptive woman. Her honest evaluation of Aunt Else's behavior was considered insightful.

If Aunt Else privately stewed about the remark, no one knew. People had other concerns. People expressed feelings, certainly, but, for the most part, they trudged on in relationships, innocent of having to worry about someone else having a nervous breakdown because of some comment. Families thrived pretty well, or so they thought, without an overdose of psychological analysis.

Clearly, this attitude toward bluntly saying what was on one's mind was part of our thinking. For example, when Joel was discharged from the Navy, he went to a clothier near the naval base. The owner had snared a lot of the Navy guys with promises of huge discounts and coupons for free shirts and ties. After years of uniforms, the men were ecstatic with the buying spree. Joel filled two suitcases, and, when we next met, he beamed with pride because of the quantity and the price.

He modeled the various jackets and suits, clearly expecting my admiration. I cringed. Although I didn't own anything vaguely resembling what was in the fashion magazines, I imagined myself as having taste. In our childhood, the Chicago newspapers were always filled with Capone-like mobsters in fedoras and checked outfits nipped in at the waist with trousers pegged at the bottom. The name for these outfits was zoot suits. Did I soft pedal my reaction? Certainly not. "You look like you're ready to be hauled off by the Feds," is what I said.

His face momentarily clouded. There was no way the clothes could be returned. Although he may have felt a double sense of shame because of his poor judgment and the waste of money, at the time my comments were shrugged off. He didn't perceive them as having sinister, deep, emotional meanings. That came much later, *after* we started attending graduate school in psychology.

Fortunately, perhaps, his turn to be objective came during that same year. My brother had been stationed near the Arctic at an Army meteorological station. In his free time, he and a few buddies went hunting. The men pooled their kill of red foxes and shipped me the pelts so I could have a fur jacket. A family friend who was a furrier made up the skins. I now owned a red fox "chubby," as they were called in the 40s.

After we moved to New York, I decided I needed something to wear with the red fox chubby and, on a walk down Broadway, we entered a women's clothing store. The saleswoman knew she had midwest innocents, and she talked me into buying a pale lime green suit with a bustle effect that she claimed had been bought and worn by the most famous actress on Broadway. I had no idea of the identity of the famed actress, but I did fall completely for her "line."

On our next outing, I wore my "actress" suit, high heels, and the red fox jacket. The reactions were astonishing. As we emerged from the subway station, Joel asked me, "Do you know why everyone was staring?"

"Not really," I admitted, rather thinking it might be the luxurious fur.

Joel offered some stunning speculations about what had attracted glances in my direction. It was probably pure luck that I wasn't picked up as a streetwalker. In thinking back, I wonder if it was the lack of make-up, somewhat unruly curly brown hair, and the dazed expression from my first subway experience that saved me. (At the time, Chicago didn't have subways.) Anyhow the fur coat and the suit, both worn only once, went into the trash can.

AMAZING BENEFITS OF GRADUATE STUDY IN PSYCHOLOGY

More importantly, it never occurred to me to obsess about any underlying meaning in *his* remarks. At least, not immediately. However, after six months of graduate education in psychology, when we had become sensitized to all the theories about people's feelings, the subtle and not-so-subtle meanings of what someone says, I lost my temper.

"What did you mean by saying I looked like a street-walker? Were you accusing me of being or becoming one? How dare you? Latent hostility, for sure. Just another of your bits of aggressive behavior reflecting a masculine ego."

He retorted, "I remember your reaction to my clothes. That was quite a guilt trip you sent me on, and you never said you were sorry. You are a castrating female."

Under the expert tutelage of professors we soon reached the point where we couldn't say anything to each other without tearing the words apart, probing for covert meanings, hunting down the implications of what was said and what might have been implied.

All of our classmates were doing the same thing. Everybody was gloriously unhappy. The professors could sense the development of the students when a member of the class would make some innocuous remark and the whole class would pounce on the innocent student, ripping apart the hidden meanings.

This was real progress. We were getting A's in our classroom work, while, at the same time, our personal relationship was becoming more and more tense. I cooked chicken one night. It wasn't done. You can't imagine what serving underdone chicken really signifies unless you have been enrolled in Psych 304, "Interpretation and analysis of subjective meanings in interpersonal relationships."

OUR HAPPINESS QUOTIENT WAS SINKING FAST

Normally talkative, we began to stutter, thinking about the implied meanings behind each word. Our fun-loving, carefree relationship quickly became heavy-handed with all the in-depth analysis. Looking back now, we wonder that we didn't choke on the words "Freudian slip," which were cited about every third sentence. Oh, how we privately sighed for the good old days when we could blurt out anything that popped into our heads without worrying about layered meanings.

In addition to Freud, we were also introduced to Carl Rogers' theories. In the late 1940s and 50s the work of Carl Rogers was exceedingly popular with many psychological educators. An important part of Roger's point of view was his emphasis on genuineness, complete and open honesty.

This is a noble goal. We suppose, if one is a saint and has only lofty thoughts, then it is probably even a good idea. But for most people, including ourselves, there are serious consequences to saying what is in your head openly and honestly. Add that to all the probing for the hidden meanings behind every remark, and if your first thought is "relationship disaster," you are *absolutely* correct.

Our arguments intensified. For example, we might start with the underdone chicken, which, at first glance, you might dismiss as a trivial issue. Let us assure you we were perilously close to separating over this matter. Keep in mind that chicken was only the stimulus for a whole chain reaction. Most arguments, as we will later discuss, begin with trivia. It's only the escalation of vituperative responses that causes major rifts.

Our argument began innocently enough. "You know I hate underdone chicken. You cooked the chicken the way I hate it. This clearly reflects a behavior which is symptomatic of your underlying rejection of me."

Serving underdone chicken was interpreted as a deliberately hostile act which I repeated over and over again to be annoying, incontrovertibly demonstrating latent hostility. By not cooking the chicken the way Joel liked it, my act was seen as a *classic* case of passive-aggression. This was the substance of his comments, said initially in a low undertone but quickly reaching a crescendo.

And my reply reflected open and genuine honesty. There was no hiding from my thoughts. Carl Rogers would have been proud of me. "You are crazy and sick. You and your family and your chicken problems. Someone in your family has an underlying bad seed."

"You call *me* crazy? You're the one that is crazy."

The simple act of undercooking chicken was now linked with implications of oedipal complexes and a variety of neuroses.

We need not tell you every detail of even one of the many infamous chicken fights that reverberated over and over again and took a dramatic turn for the worse with the second half of the course about Rogerian honesty, Freud's hidden meanings and the rest of the people whose works we dutifully studied.

The chicken business became the focus of what was called latent hostility, or inconsiderate behavior, and could be traced to a mother who also had rejected her son's desires about favorite foods. Oh, we were really, genuinely communicating now.

In reality, there was a simple answer which was not accepted and which was more difficult to verbalize. I didn't care much for cooking and, if I was hungry, I couldn't wait until the chicken was done. A good counterattack on my part such as, "Why don't you cook the damn chicken yourself?" didn't help because we had made a pact that I would cook and Joel would clean up, a pact we have kept over all these decades.

It was at that point, when we were feeling depressed at the disintegration of our relationship and wrongly assuming it was the stress of too little money and no set careers, that we took stock of the situation. The next brilliant set of insights gradually began to evolve. Obviously, as with any great ideas, it took time, years even, for these insights to be refined, clarified, and researched.

In essence the core idea was simply this: *More communication is not always better.*

A great deal of psychological thinking has been focused on discussions and research in an effort to demonstrate that happy human relationships are positively correlated with open, forthright, in-depth communication. Thus, a lot of time and energy is directed toward getting people to communicate, explore feelings, describe their feelings and, generally, to be expressive in a variety of ways.

For example, there are marital encounter sessions where couples can go and bare their souls, let it all spill out, tell more, reveal more. Countless publications and articles stress the importance of communication, cautioning couples that marriage survival is linked to a couple's ability to communicate. Husbands and wives must be open and genuine with their thoughts and feelings.

Americans are at the forefront in the contention that communication is the be all and end all of marital relationships. Not every society holds this belief. While in graduate school, we picked up extra money tutoring. One of our pupils was a stunning lady from Shanghai who had married an American whom she had met when he was working in China. Our job was to teach her English so that she and her husband could communicate verbally.

Class sessions began with a hunt for the books which she kept in a locked cupboard. It took at least half an hour before she would reluctantly produce the key. The next half hour was spent ordering lunch. We had been hired by the husband who had explained to us that he wanted his wife to learn English because, now that they were living in New York, her social skills at company affairs and dinner parties was important to his career.

It didn't take more than a few sessions for us to discover that this gorgeous woman, wearing breathtaking Oriental outfits, who caused all traffic to stop as we walked in midtown

Manhattan, spoke *perfect* English, not with our flat midwestern vowels but with an impeccable British accent.

One afternoon, taking me aside, she patted my hand and told me I was making a terrible mistake talking so much to my husband. "No mystery," she said. "You will tire of each other. To know more of the other takes a lifetime. Why hurry? A little bit each year, no more." She even hinted that she might speak to my husband privately. He, too, was erring and could use some help.

Before we go into further discussion, let us assure you we really do value and appreciate communication as a process leading to greater understanding. We are not abandoning all of the basic beliefs about the importance of communication. We just think the basic concepts need some strong modification.

In every marriage, every relationship, obviously there's a time to listen with empathic understanding. However, just as wisely as one learns to listen, there are times when the example of the famed monkey figurines in front of a temple in Japan should be taken to heart. "See no evil, hear no evil, and speak no evil."

We definitely aren't proposing a check on communication; however, what our studies of married couples as well as thinking through our own relationship have demonstrated is that, in every marriage, crises may result from *too much* of a basically good idea.

QUALITY, IN-DEPTH, GOOD COMMUNICATION DOES NOT NECESSARILY MEAN MORE, BUT CAN MEAN LESS

There can be too much openness and too much overly sensitive analysis. Everything couples say to each other doesn't necessarily have deep, shadowy meanings. Maybe sometimes what we say is simply a passing thought, blurted out unthinkingly, that should be left to rest. Maybe there are other times when our honest thoughts are better left *unsaid*. Not every cast-away remark should be probed to its limit. Not every statement needs a response. Not everything in your head needs to be said.

First, let's look at the central notion that more communication is not necessarily better. Our research and the research of one of our graduate students dramatically demonstrates that marriages can and do suffer from too much sensitivity.

The original study identified a group of very happily married couples, and a group of unhappily married couples on the verge of separation or divorce. These two groups of couples were studied in terms of their abilities to communicate emotionally with each other.

Initially, following conventional psychological wisdom, all of us fully expected to find that the happily married couples would be more emotionally sensitive to each other. After all, doesn't marital advice consistently proclaim that being emotionally sensitive to each other is a good thing? Women and men all talk about wanting a partner in life who is sensitive, caring, *in tune* with their emotional needs.

Much to everyone's surprise the results were totally out-of-line with our expectations. By and large, the unhappily married couples proved to be *far more* sensitive to each other's emotional expression than were the happily married couples. Repeated studies revealed identical findings.

There were two scores, one for happiness and love or positive feelings, and one score for unpleasant, negative feelings, for example, anger and anxiety. In analyzing the data, we found that the two groups didn't differ very much in their sensitivity to *positive* feelings. That is, regardless of whether the couples were happily or unhappily married they were in tune or sensitive to each other's feelings of joy and happiness. The big difference came in terms of the unhappily married couples' sensitivity to negative feelings. The unhappily married couples were tuned in to each other's anger and anxiety much more than the happily married couples.

As a result, the unhappily married couples tended to interpret their spouse's behavior in more negative emotional terms and this contributed to the discomfort of their marital relations. In contrast, the happily married couples were much less aware of the negative feelings in the relationship.

SELECTIVE INSENSITIVITY

We could readily see the effects of this in our own relationship. For the most part, we were happy together. However, when one or the other was angry or anxious and the other empathized too much, was too much aware, the unhappiness quotient of our relationship spiraled upwards. We discovered that when one of us was upset it was far better to be a little less in tune.

By incorporating this principle into our marriage, we have been able to survive a lot of crises. If there's a problem and both of us become anxious, angry, and tense, then we both feel as if we are drowning. It's far more productive to exercise a little selective insensitivity, to take the other's unhappiness a little less personally.

There's an old cliché that it takes two to tango. If one person is angry, and the other person becomes angry too, disgruntled words fly. If one or the other is very sad, then it isn't very helpful for both to feel the same intensity of sadness. We're emphatically not proposing that communication halt. We firmly believe in confidences between couples, sharing of experiences, supportive behavior and words, the personal and rewarding touches that can only come through shared communication.

But there are important times when *more is not better*. There can be too much openness, too much communication. Not every word the other person says needs an answer. "The chicken isn't done," doesn't need a snappy reply. Not every word that is said has some long history that needs to be analyzed. And, even if there is a true Freudian slip, you might ask yourself, in terms of the overall relationship, does it really serve any purpose to probe all the hidden meanings? Perhaps, rather than thinking about the great retort, the response that will put the other person in his or her place, it might be far more productive to keep in mind that more is not always better. *Selective insensitivity definitely is an important giant step toward restoring marital happiness.*

DON'T MAKE EMOTIONAL MOUNTAINS OUT OF MOODY MOLEHILLS

A corollary to the overall insight that more communication isn't always better is our realization of the inherent dangers in making *emotional mountains from moody molehills*. This idea was generated in a number of different ways. The first awareness came when we did a study of divorced couples and couples about to begin the divorce process. All were desperate to get out of a less than satisfying relationship, a relationship which, of course, involved poor communication. In fact, one major reason that most couples identify as propelling them into divorce is the lack of understanding communication.

While interviewing the couples at length, we realized that, almost without exception, one or the other regularly zeroed in on the moody, unresponsive behavior of the other person. "There are times when to drag a word from him is worse than pulling a tooth. There's no real give and take in what we say to each other," said one woman.

"We're not on the same wavelength," said one man. He confessed that they had a lot going for the relationship, but that it drove him batty when she turned "sour."

As he described the situation, "I come in from work. She's got that long face on. What about my day? OK, she's been at work, too. So we greet each other with these faces, and I can hear her going into the bathroom, running the shower, not even bothering to say one damn word to me. I could be some brick wall, some fixture to be knocked down and propped up only when she wanted it that way. Did you ever try to have a conversation with a stone wall?"

"How often," we asked, "does this behavior occur?"

"Often enough."

"And in between these awful bouts?"

"She's fine," he admitted. "Great. But you know, I've reached the end point. She's got some crazy notion that she alone has the right to have bad days. I have mine, too. If I ask her what's up, the answer can be a verbal slap in the face."

The vicious cycle begins quite innocently. A spouse has a pouting expression.

"Anything the matter?" asks the other person.

That's precisely the spark that is needed to get the exchange off the ground.

Couples sometimes behave as if they are tigers in the jungle waiting for the prey to appear before moving in for the kill. Every blip, every sad face, every less than joyful remark, every little dip in emotional good humor, every lack of exchange is interpreted as hostility, rejection, defensiveness, neurosis, inferiority complex, or anxiety, and all are taken very personally.

It was surprising to us how many of the almost divorced and divorced couples were *unable* to cite a dramatic turning point that drove them apart. More often than not the break came because of what we call making emotional mountains out of moody molehills.

*A LITTLE "TIME OUT" IN COMMUNICATION
CAN GO A LONG WAY*

Adults often fail to understand this behavior in themselves. We did, too. Only after we had children did we begin to understand how not paying attention, not exaggerating, not contributing to the mood swings of a teenager, could make all the difference not only for the youngster's sanity but for our own.

All of us are subject to mood swings. These are normal. We can't and do not face the world everyday with a huge grin and a carefree demeanor. We have our ups and downs. We see this in children. We know this happens, all too frequently, in teenagers. What we forget is that adults are not any different. Yes, it would be nice if one had perfect control and could hide all the subtle and not-so-subtle swings of temperament, but most of us can't. And, in a marriage, when one or the other spouse gets down and displaces some of his or her own tense feelings onto the other person there's the potential for a crisis.

There are rarely any problems between couples in the peak periods. The crises come when emotions spiral down. What is the right response when a spouse is "sour?" With children, parents know exactly how to handle the situation. The overtired child who acts out and refuses to settle down is shunted off to a bedroom or quiet space for a cooling-off period. "Time out" is a favorite device used by parents and educators to handle those "tough" moments.

We all need our quiet times, cooling-off periods to give us a chance to regroup. Communication at these times only gets in the way, serves as a springboard for a lot of give and take, words that would be better left unspoken. Learning to distinguish between the moody molehills and the things that are really important is a challenge worth considering. In any case, the time to discuss the source of the mood, the root of the problem, is not until the mood has passed and emotions on both sides are under control once more.

It probably is better to err on the safe side—a little drawing back rather than a probing, plunging forward. In time, the mood will pass; the argument about underdone chicken will fade, the hairs left in the bathroom sink will be forgotten, the long face at the end of the day or the harsh words, "I don't want to talk about it," should be accepted and not over-interpreted. Refusing to make an emotional mountain from what is merely a transient molehill will be an important step toward the longevity of your marriage.

SECOND THOUGHTS ABOUT HONEST AND GENUINE COMMUNICATION

Finally, in an era concerned with morality, we will approach the last corollary to the "more is not always better" communication insight with a great deal of caution. The issue is honesty and genuineness. None of you want to be married, or to stay married to someone who is not *wholly truthful*. After all, there's enough deception in the world without adding more of the same within one's own marriage. Above all, couples have to be honest with each other. They have to tell the truth. White lies grow into dark, foreboding lies. Lies are discovered. Trust is lost.

However, in summing up all we have learned about this insight that more communication is not always better, we have to add that honest and open genuineness must be tempered with kindness. In discussions with couples about this point we are often challenged,

"In effect, you are telling us to lie."

"Well, not exactly to lie."

"Then what is it?"

"A little graying around the edge, perhaps. Not a lie."

Our contention is that, at *certain critical times*, being brutally frank, directly honest, can only raise the rate of tension, making attack and counterattack inevitable.

All of us have our weak spots, areas where we are especially vulnerable and sensitive. Certain subjects, certain issues can trigger the worst in a person. When couples marry, they may or may not be aware of these trigger points, but they learn quickly. It's not that these subjects have to be avoided, but, when they are considered, they have to be approached with a little sensitive understanding. There's nothing earthshaking in this concept.

What is unbelievable is how many couples, *including* ourselves, quickly lose sight of this fact. Any stress, any tension, and we zero in on those trigger-sensitive areas, sometimes without even realizing what we are doing. We've seen countless examples like this one. The wife has a long-standing complaint:

"We didn't live together before we were married. Every time we were together, he was impeccably groomed. To be honest, I felt he was more put together than I was. Now I know we're all human, but I was shocked after we were married to discover he was a slob. You know what a chair means to him—a place to dump his clothes instead of putting them in the laundry basket."

And the husband has his own gripe. "She uses credit cards as if they were play money. OK, so she brings home a paycheck equal to mine. OK, so she got a fat bonus. So what? We have a joint account. I can't see the spending patterns helping us save for retirement."

Now, generally this husband and wife were quite content with each other. Their happiness score was well above average. However, when there was any sort of tension, any crisis whatsoever, no matter the subject, the final bitter words centered on his messy behavior and her spending habits.

Married couples are determined to change each other, and *some* change may occur. However, as we discovered in our marriage, there are certain stubborn, unchangeable, fixed, rooted, trigger-sensitive areas that are *cemented* into a person's psyche. We could begin an argument *today* about something innocuous and, if that argument continues to escalate, somehow or another we will end up with underdone chicken, an argument that had its genesis more than fifty years ago.

These sensitive areas, we believe, are learned early in life and are *stubbornly* resistant to change. The best we can do is treat them as a virus and keep them dormant, subdued with as much verbal antibiotics as we can dole out. Now this doesn't mean that, in quiet, reflective times, the wife can't bring up the mess on the chair that drives her up the wall, or the shaving hairs not wiped from the bathroom sink, nor does he have to shy away from all money discussions.

It's just that couples must never forget the vulnerability of the other person in *certain areas*. The best that can be done is to remind oneself about these areas and to be somewhat less than direct and forthright, at least at sensitive times. We are shocked to realize, in our own psyches, *five decades later*, how some basic quirks are still basic quirks. Age hasn't done much to effect change. Our edges or sensitivities might be a little smoother, but even today there are certain areas that remain red-flagged as danger zones for us. That is why we suggest that open, genuine, honest, truthful communication between spouses must be tempered by kindness and understanding.

We believe all of these corollaries are entwined together: *selective insensitivity, avoidance of making emotional mountains out of moody molehills, tempering openness and genuineness with kindness*. The scenario for each of you will be unique; however, the general principle that more communication is not always better holds true for all of us.

4 MoneyMatters

"They're very unhappy, miserable people," my grand-mother reassured me the day I gave her a detailed report about a rich family and all the wonderful things *that* granddaughter received for her birthday.

I asked innocently, "Why aren't they happy?"

In a very knowing voice which boded no challenge, she replied, "You will learn in life that *money does not buy happiness.*"

We were children of the Depression. The family's economic base had been devastated. Therefore, it is not surprising that our early attitudes toward money were a trifle skewed. Like many others of our generation we grew up believing, or at least very familiar with, certain platitudes. For example, the notion that money cannot purchase happiness (a thought to make everyone less unhappy about their economic losses); we also heard that money doesn't grow on trees (meaning you have to work hard for money); that rich people squeeze money (meaning rich people took money away from the rest of us, were always more demanding than less affluent individuals and that's how they became rich in the first place); that rich people burn money (meaning they are terribly wasteful and not nearly as prudent as the rest of mankind); and, finally, that rich people wear their money (meaning they have to show off their wealth in jewelry and clothing just to make others miserable).

Sorting out the accuracy from all the folk wisdom about money is definitely not an easy task. In actuality, we have always had doubts about the validity of these so-called truisms. The first time we seriously questioned the idea that money can't buy happiness occurred one Sunday evening during our first term in graduate school.

We were desperate for a pint of coffee ice cream, a tantalizing flavor we had never encountered growing up in Chicago. Within a short time of our arrival in New York, coffee ice cream rapidly became a serious contender for first-place addiction replacing the infamous orange Lifesavers. The problem blocking our happiness was *money*. We were without any.

For an entire hour we scrounged through every pocket, emptied briefcases, crawled around the floor, and searched every corner, including the space under the radiator, hoping to find stray coins. The hunt was painful. All we could come up with was fifteen cents: enough, we hoped, for *half* a pint. Scurrying down to the corner delicatessen on Broadway, we were chagrined to discover we were pennies short. The remainder of the evening was wasted. You could not have convinced us then that money doesn't buy happiness.

Luckily our GI check arrived the next day. One hundred and five dollars, it had to last the month. Cashing the check we dined at the university cafeteria and hurried over to satisfy our craving. Much to our astonishment, we no longer had the remaining 103 dollars. With a gasp of horror we realized we had lost the wad of bills in the cafeteria.

Hopelessly we returned to the university and talked to the cashier.

Yes, she told us, she had a sum of money. Could we tell her how much money was in the folded wad?

"One hundred and three dollars, the remainder of our GI check."

She handed us our money. An unknown veteran (the university was packed with them), had given the money to the cashier saying, "I know how the person must feel. Probably what he had to live on for the month."

Money can't buy happiness? At that stage in our lives you couldn't have convinced us of the truth of that tired old myth.

As we learned even before our weekend honeymoon was over, money is the root cause of many marital conflicts. Questions of whether to save or spend it, of what to give up when there's simply not enough of it for everything, and of who makes the daily decisions about how much gets spent for what, can all cause crises in any marital relationship from time to time. This concern is quite easy to understand. Money is necessary to live on, not only to buy bus tickets or coffee ice cream, but also for life's real necessities. Unfortunately, while most couples have visions of the lifestyles they want to have in the future, they don't often discuss financial plans or goals before they marry.

For example, let's describe a pre-marriage date where the woman shows up in an expensive outfit, with new shoes she hardly needs. The man arrives in an equally costly jacket, shirt, and necktie. After he expresses his undying love, it would be unthinkable for him to break into conversation with some comment such as, "That's a helluva lot you spent on something to wear for *one* evening. I hope this doesn't continue after we marry."

And, it is equally unlikely that the woman would counter by commenting on his absurdly high-priced jacket and tie, cautioning him that she will never sacrifice her desire for a well-kept home to his fashion sense. Besides, since she earns her own salary, she intends to spend what she wants, and on whatever she pleases.

In fact, other than extremely wealthy couples who make sure they sign pre-nuptial agreements to protect their individual assets, by and large, regular people would consider money conversations *before* marriage "tacky."

The situation changes radically after marriage. In one of our studies, couples were given lists of topics and asked to keep a record of their conversations for a two-week period by checking off the topic discussed and the approximate amount of time spent in discussion. We also asked a group of singles who were dating someone on a regular basis to perform the same task.

Just as we expected, money was seldom, if ever, a major subject of conversation among the singles other than some exploration of grandiose dreams about making millions, more often than not, said facetiously. However, for the marrieds, *regardless* of the length of the marriage, a totally different picture emerged. Money was not only the *most frequently* cited topic for discussion, it also took up the most time. One woman wryly noted, "We can spend forty minutes talking about money to every minute talking about love and romance. This wasn't the way it was, I can tell you, before we married."

The inescapable reality is that affairs of money are an ongoing potential source of crisis in every marriage. Unchecked, money matters have the possibility of becoming a *major* source of conflict. These very strong words are not meant to upset or frighten you. We must keep in mind that famous and rich people have had to face similar problems. It may comfort you to know that John F. Kennedy was frantic, often irate, about Jackie's expenditures on clothing. Evidently he worked tirelessly trying to curb her purchases. The Queen of England chastised Prince Charles as a young man for his wanton carelessness and total disregard for the value of money. According to news reports, he had lost a dog's collar that cost a couple of pounds.

Because of the widespread arguments about money, advice columns, marriage advisors, and other consultants have come up with all sorts of solutions designed to help couples avoid marital crises about finances. Couples, for example, are urged to draw up budgets and make detailed plans about how to handle their income. Supposedly categorizing expenses will relieve tension and prevent disagreements.

Parents are encouraged to teach young children the value and importance of money through giving them allowances. One of our cousins followed this advice. His child, delving into the clothing budget, bought too much bubble gum and for one month wore socks with holes. The intent of these messages is to provide useful instruction at an early age. Hopefully, when the youngsters become adults with their own families and responsibilities, they will know how to handle their incomes sensibly.

Please be assured that it is not our intent to demean any of these solutions. They can be important and useful tools to help couples avoid the pitfalls of acrimony because of money. Any suggestion that has the potential of averting major crises and shouting matches is worth considering.

LOOK AT MONEY FROM A COMPLETELY DIFFERENT PERSPECTIVE

However, with all due respect for those plans and approaches to money issues, we do not believe they really solve the basic problems. In contrast, we believe the following personal insights, based on observations and our long marital history, not only provide dramatically different solutions but, more importantly, present the topic from a whole new perspective.

UNCHANGEABLE ATTITUDES

Our first insight was that attitudes toward money are learned *very early* in life. No amount of income or financial success ever really changes an individual's attitudes. Ingrained beliefs are forever. The *most* that any couple can do is work with or around these early learned attitudes as best they can.

We have observed an orthopedic surgeon, who grew up in a poor family but now makes a million dollars a year, playing tennis with a battered tennis racket, worn sneakers, and a shirt one step away from tatters. Every dollar spent by his wife and children for so-called luxuries is exceedingly painful to him. Try as the family does, nothing can convince this man that he is not one step away from the poverty line.

One young wife has a husband who works extremely hard to make a living. He thoughtfully puts away IRAs and is already saving for college tuitions for his three-year-old twins. She, on the other hand, concerned about her image in the community, has insisted they buy a Mercedes sports car and a BMW sedan. Raised as the darling of a prosperous family, her every want was satisfied. She has never changed.

As for us, we are at opposite ends of the spectrum when it comes to money attitudes. Joel is indifferent, casual, unconcerned. Rarely, if ever, does he worry about money. Of course, he enjoys what money buys, but to him, making a big issue of expenses or going to extreme lengths to acquire material possessions seems pointless, hurtful, and self-serving.

His attitudes were formed by his father, a financially successful man who made a big point of giving young Joel lessons in economics. For example, he kept a careful tally of every cent Joel cost the family. He insisted Joel bank *all* of his part-time earnings from packing cough drops in his senior year of high school to defray the costs of college. The lesson Joel learned from all of this—one of total indifference to all money matters—was probably not what his father intended, but it has stuck with him for life.

I, on the other hand, learned my sensible, conservative, practical attitudes toward money in my early childhood. Memories of Depression stories, including stories of my grandmothers who valiantly tried to retrieve their life savings from a "locked" neighborhood bank, served to make me cautious. My father's own loss of considerable property reinforced the lesson.

It would be unthinkable for me to go to a very elegant restaurant, *even as a guest*, and not look for the least expensive item on the menu, perhaps a simple pasta or chicken dish, while resenting and envying those who order "quail under glass" with casual indifference. Purchases for Joel bring elation, but anything bought for myself induces guilt.

Knowing the other person's predisposition about money can be of immeasurable help when it comes to crises about money matters. For example, when we do something quite luxurious I have to wade through the guilt and the apologies before accepting the pleasure. In the beginning, we would fight about my Scrooge-ish mentality. Now Joel has learned that no amount of money we earn can change my basic attitude. Therefore, rather than trying to argue me out of my guilt, he tries to soothe and assuage the guilt, often to the extent of blaming himself for any and all wanton expenditures.

I, on the other hand, knowing how cavalier and indifferent Joel is about money, have taken *full* charge of the checking account, carefully monitoring what we spend. When questioned about our assets, I always reduce them by at least one third which makes him a trifle more cautious and keeps us solvent.

It might be noted that the job of handling money which I have taken on is very much the style for wives in many different places. For example, in general, the Japanese culture reflects considerable male chauvinism. By and large, husbands are not involved in childcare or other domestic matters. Married women who have children *rarely* work outside the home. And yet, in that society, the vast majority of married women control *all* the family finances. Men turn over their full salaries to their wives who decide what to do with the money. Husbands are given spending money for the week.

The pattern of women in charge of family finances is also true of a number of areas in Africa where market women, for example, will manage all the money. Often their husbands are grateful to receive allowances or have to "forget" to report some wages or private earnings to their wives in order to have some personal spending money.

A number of women in our studies talked about keeping personal accounts for their salaries. Although finances can be kept separate, some money must be pooled for general family expenses. The responsibility for this category usually falls to one or the other spouse. It's not always possible for two people to confer about every household expenditure. Thus, for the sake of ease, one or the other spouse usually finds it easier and more convenient to take charge of general household expenditures.

We are definitely not lobbying for every wife to have total control of family finances. You will have to work out the solution that is *best* for the two of you. However, the invaluable insight that whatever you do is going to be conditioned by attitudes you have learned very early in life will help you tolerate a spouse's quirks and delegate responsibility for financial matters in ways that reduce the opportunity for quarrels and accusations about money.

We expect that as you consider some of your recent tussles over money matters, it will become clear that one of you is more cautious about spending while the other is less inhibited. Perhaps one of you is always more concerned that there be enough to cover all the necessaries while the other seems to simply take it on faith that the family will not starve.

In the interest of marital harmony (and solvency, too), it may make sense to give the checkbook and the credit cards to the more conservative spender. Or perhaps all that person needs is total control over the savings account.

Whatever your solution, simply being aware of your own and your spouse's attitudes toward money will go a long way toward reducing the emotional impact of any future money battles.

Also, be aware of the times when your typical attitudes shift, when the free spender suddenly gets cautious and the risk-averse throws caution to the wind. This shifting from conservative to free wheeler frequently happens for us when we move out of our familiar environment on trips. When we travel, Joel handles the money. I immediately become a spender, choosing the "right" hotels, and generally spending with a carefree attitude. The principle we have learned is that *whoever handles the money tends to be more tightfisted than the other person.* Therefore, it is a good idea to exchange roles occasionally to get a real sense of what your spouse is experiencing emotionally.

THE SECOND INSIGHT

No matter how much you earn, other people are going to have more. This fact of life usually won't bother you as long as the other people are public figures, famous individuals, Hollywood or TV stars whom you are most unlikely to encounter. It only becomes a problem when the other people are your peers. For example, when we play tennis on public courts with a dress-down group wearing every kind of attire from red spandex running shorts to black oversized jeans, we are totally relaxed, as is everyone else. Side court conversations are casual, always about the game, the weather, or a great new pair of tennis shoes.

The atmosphere is significantly different at clubs. When we play in private facilities there are signs posted everywhere about "proper attire." Side court conversations rattle on about the latest and most expensive equipment, the newest and most fashionable tennis outfits, and the current cost of club memberships.

Even if your family has managed beautifully with an ordinary bathtub and shower, being invited over to visit a relative who has just installed a separate Jacuzzi area with spray shower heads coming out every which way from all four walls is bound to cause some unrest. Unchecked, the discomforts elicited by envy have an insidious way of spilling over and maturing into crisis arguments.

We feel the best way to handle this matter is simply *avoidance*. Be a bit more selective about your friends. When we were in graduate school everyone we knew paid two dollars for a chance to stand at the rear of the main floor of the Metropolitan Opera house. Occasionally, someone sitting in the upholstered seats would get a stomachache or some such thing and rush out. That meant one of us had a great seat for the rest of the performance. No one was envious. No one begrudged the one nearest the seat the right to occupancy. Have-nots hanging out with have-nots rarely causes money problems within the family.

It's only when your friends are outdistancing you that tension begins to rear its ugly little head. Sometimes the source of discomfort comes from unwitting comparisons. We recall, for example, early in our teaching careers, being invited to another faculty home. The wife, we had been told, inherited immense wealth, a way of explaining to us that we should be prepared for a home and lifestyle quite unlike what was familiar to the rest of us.

The dinner was lovely. Everyone had his or her own matched chair, instead of stools dragged in from back rooms. The dishes were perfectly coordinated. However, what really intrigued me was the shining, polished table which I was pleased to note was the same color and had the same high sheen as the one we had just bought the previous week.

I noted, "The table is lovely!"

The wife smiled and said, "Thank you," eyes modestly closing.

I should have stopped while I was ahead. However, I was kind of excited and, in all innocence, continued, "We just bought a new *Formica* table, too."

Her silence was stunning. I remember watching her hands play with the dinner knife.

"Lois, my dear, this is Widdicomb—*not* Formica."

Having her table worth *thousands* compared to our forty-five dollar Formica did not sit well with our hostess. We did not return the invitation nor did she include us in any other dinner parties. Over the years, we have been amazed at the effort people have put forth to impress us with their financial status or possessions. No one seems to buy just a car; one buys an expensive, big car. No one buys just a house. They buy oversized, extensive, costly residences with many bedrooms and bathrooms.

It's not that we escaped from all this comparison. We had our upmanship tactics as well; however, Joel's indifference to such material issues and money did have an affect on our sons. There was one very rewarding moment that occurred when the boys were about ten and six. Some rich friends came to visit, and the husband told our sons that *if* they washed their hands and faces and promised *not* to jump around he would give them a ride in his new Cadillac.

"Why would I want to ride in your Cadillac?" asked Mickey, our older boy. "My dad has a car."

Although it is impossible to check out the incomes of everyone you meet, you will discover many of your marital arguments will drop off if you somehow find out the financial status of people before developing long friendships. Beware of those whom you meet who lose no time hinting at their income bracket and regaling you with stories about their recent luxury purchases. You're only headed for marital trouble. We are not advocating escapism. It is just that the "keeping up with the Jones's" mentality can all too often get in the way of more productive activities.

Do what you can with what you have and *always live under your income*. This advice will not only keep you solvent but will go a long way toward preventing marital discord. Of course, this plan will only work well when each of you keeps firmly entrenched in your mind your own personal hang-ups about money.

No matter how much you have or earn, after you have a home and children, you will need a minimum of 10 to 20 percent more money to meet expenses. Knowing this valuable bit of information, which we might note took us many decades to fully appreciate, you will never be horrified, surprised, angry, disturbed, or disconsolate to discover there is no money left at the end of the month. Imagine never again having to sit, head in your hands, bemoaning the horror of what has happened and how you are going to have to scrimp and save until balance is restored to a bank account. There never will be such a crisis, because you will expect to have trouble making ends meet from the beginning.

Prior to having children and a home of our own, we managed beautifully, traveling all over the world on five dollars a day. Our travel dress was casual, our diet plain, and our hotel requirements minimal. Only one person ever felt concerned about us. We were in Copenhagen one year at the same time as an educational conference. Standing outside our hotel, we saw the President of Teachers College, Columbia University, whom we didn't know personally, arrive in a car. On a lark we introduced ourselves as graduate students. He was gracious but in a hurry and rushed off. However, minutes later he came running back out of the building, a worried look on his face. "Are you kids OK? Do you have enough money? Call me if you need anything." He handed us a card with his phone number.

Children and a home mark the end of a balanced budget. One fall we were feeling rather smug. Prep school tuitions were all nicely stashed away in a savings account. Our checking account was solvent. We were doing just fine until we stood in our bedroom and were lightly misted with rain. The house needed a new roof.

It seems that every time everything is in the "black" in the checkbook, the appliances, lying in wait for just such a moment, emerge from their shadows, like lions stalking prey, and promptly disintegrate. We owned a camper VW van and faithfully paid loan installments for three years. When the last payment was finally made, the notice went up to sell the van and a buyer came.

The van's transmission failed at the moment of delivery.

No matter how much you have, the size of your bonus, the extra consultant fees that come your way, you will always need 10 to 20 percent more to really live at the same standard. Of course, as you move up the financial ladder, your wants increase. Wants are always one step ahead. One can never catch up with wants, so it is important to resign yourself.

Our children helped teach us this lesson. Although there are four years between them, our sons' birthdays are only a week apart with Valentine's Day in between. One year we decided on a joint celebration. We came up with a great plan to buy everything imaginable and fill the dining room with mounds of boxes. We did not spare expense. Bicycles, hockey sticks, games, balls, bats were wrapped with consummate care and placed beneath "Happy Birthday" banners. The boys were overwhelmed. For once we assumed their wants would be satisfied.

Each present was quickly opened, exclaimed over, and put aside, and the wrapping of the next package attacked. They were soon finished.

"Is that all?" asked one son. So much for satisfied desire.

Couples rarely are in accord on how much should be spent, where, and for what. One sees the yard as having priority; the other wants to redo the bedroom with French Provincial furniture. One spouse thinks swimming pool, the other wall-to-wall carpeting for the playroom, foyer, and staircase.

The ensuing arguments follow a rather set routine of attack and counterattack. "My husband," one woman reported, " will spend 100 dollars on a bottle of wine, but when I tell him I'm getting new towels he argues that our towels aren't torn, and besides he loves green. He says this just because he knows I've decided to change the bathroom color scheme to yellow."

We do not advocate a laissez-faire attitude toward money. Obviously sensible planning is crucial in today's world; however, what must be guarded against is the bickering and quarreling that can drive a wedge between spouses. *Hopefully, our insights will make the difference.* Once you recognize and truly understand that children are going to be an unending cost; that, no matter what you make, you will always need 10 to 20 percent more income to make ends really meet; that your wants go on and on; that selecting the wrong kinds of friends can be a disaster; that it is important to live *below* your income, *not above*; that one or the other of you will *always* be critical about the other's spending habits; you are going to be astonished and rapturous to observe how money arguments will evaporate.

It has taken us many years to identify these insights. We did not know them in our early years of marriage. A stranger tried to help us out one time. We were attending national meetings of the American Psychological Association. Joel had presented a well-received paper. However, rather than attend the lovely expensive dinner afterward, we went to a coffee shop and sat at the counter eating tuna salad sandwiches and scrambled eggs (the least costly items on the menu). A man sitting on an adjoining stool started to chat with us. We bubbled over with information about the meetings and Joel's performance.

"Why are you eating here?"

"Oh," we replied, in our martyr mode, "we didn't want to spend the money."

"Do you have the money?"

"Well, yes, but . . ."

"Just don't forget," he told us, "There will be no pockets in your shrouds."

5 Identity, Individuality, and Interdependence

The first major psychological crisis of marriage involves forging a *new* marital identity. This includes the identity of each spouse in relation to the other person, and the identity of the married couple in relation to the rest of the world.

A frightening thought, isn't it? Although a marriage ceremony doesn't take very long, perhaps as long as an hour or as brief as ten minutes, in many significant ways, it has the potential to turn lives upside-down. That certainly happened to us. Our pre-marriage identities were thrown off balance. We married for a good reason, fun and games, and suddenly we were faced with having to work out a whole new identity *within the context of the marriage.*

Our individualism was dramatically threatened. We couldn't think of ourselves as individuals anymore. There was a couple to consider. It's a stunning, unnerving shock. When our egos were threatened, we responded in a very normal fashion by digging our heels in, ready to do anything and everything to preserve who we thought we were as individuals. Our behavior and reactions were quite typical. Every couple, in one way or another, has to face this same marriage identity crisis.

One young woman whom we interviewed has been happily married to the same man for some fifteen years. She recalls her second thoughts about the marriage after a stunning wedding and a glamorous reception.

"We checked into an absolutely fantastic island hotel for our honeymoon. The manager called us 'Mr. and Mrs.' In that split second, I realized I had lost my name. I was no longer me. I wanted out. I had this awful feeling my whole past was wiped away. Somebody else was in my skin ready to begin life over again with a 'stranger.'

"I didn't like it one bit. I wasn't only scared. I was *uncomfortable*. No one likes to give up who they are just like that— with a snap of the fingers. The name was symbolic. It's different for guys. Suddenly a whole chain reaction of second thoughts about what I had done came into my head."

LIFE'S JUST NOT THE SAME AFTER MARRIAGE.
YOU DEFINITELY ARE NOT THE SAME PERSON AS YOU WERE
BEFORE IN THE EYES OF THE WORLD.

After we were married I went back to finish my senior year at the University of Michigan. When Joel returned to his naval base to complete his tour of duty, his old buddies backed off in a number of small but significant ways. For example, he wasn't asked to hang out with the others on Saturday nights.

"What's the problem?"

"No problem."

"Then what gives?"

"Oh, you know, you're married now," they mumbled.

The message was quite loud and clear. A barrier had been set up between the single and the married guys. Joel suddenly belonged to the latter group. He had been initiated into another world, much like what happens in primitive tribes when single men and single women occupy dwellings away from the main clan until they marry.

Joel suspects that even his assignments changed. The implicit feeling was that certain adventuresome, interesting assignments belonged to single guys who didn't have the responsibilities that came with a wife and a future family. In subtle ways, his naval wings were clipped.

I was equally taken aback when I returned to the campus, ready to finish my last two semesters for a bachelor's degree, planning to share the same living quarters with my "old" college roommate. We had roomed together amicably for three years and expected to do so for one more.

I had no idea that my new role, officially registered at the University of Michigan student office, would send one of the deans of women into a panic. I was summoned immediately and told to clear out and find some place else to live.

"But I've lived there for three years. I paid my deposit for this last year."

She looked at me with an amazed, "I can't believe you are for real" kind of expression.

"Have you no idea of who you are and what your status is?"

"I'm a senior. My name is Lois Leiderman Davitz. I married a guy named Joel."

"Yes, that's precisely the problem."

I remained confused, feeling much like a first grader who has squashed gum under a desk and now faces a principal's disciplinary action.

With a sigh of irritation, this "mature" dean of a major university, who maintained honor among the coeds and made sure they returned to the dorms before 10:30 p.m. on weekdays, stared me down. (Just imagine a dean trying to pull this power play with a 90s student.)

"You are a married woman," she retorted, making little effort to conceal her skepticism. "University policy is that married women and single women cannot live in the same residence hall. You are a different person."

"I'm not." I fairly shouted my response. "I am the same person." It really churned my stomach to think I was someone else simply because of that Justice of the Peace. The thought was intolerable. Joel and I got married. How could that turn me, chameleon-like, into another person?

"My roommate knows my husband. He's not going to be living with us. I can't see what's so wrong."

It finally dawned on me that her major concern was that somehow, my new identity might contaminate my former roommate, as well as other girls in the house.

"I swear I won't say anything. I will never talk about the 'new' me," I promised, hoping my acceptance of a new identity would pacify her.

"All we ever talk about anyway," I assured her, "are school subjects like economics, political science, and calculus."

It took a number of high-level meetings and earnest pleas from my former roommate before we had permission to occupy the same quarters. I was closely monitored by the house mother with reports to the dean, and it took a special waiver for me to get permission to return to the dorm late after a weekend when Joel came to visit.

No couple escapes this first jolt having to do with their new identity. The first worry comes from feeling you're *giving up* something. The second concern is wondering *who you are* in this new relationship. What we have learned over the years, however, is that no identity is inflexible.

The identities we were so sure we had forged before marriage have, without even our awareness, inevitably and dramatically changed in many ways over time. We have spoken to many singles who talk about wanting to find out *who they are* before they enter marriage as if who they are is going to be a constant. That just doesn't happen, even with the best of intentions and the most concerted effort.

Identity, we have discovered, is clearly a matter of time and place. Of course, there are certain "cores" to every individual. However, notwithstanding the core attributes or characteristics that make you who you are, the indisputable fact is that identity changes are inevitable over the course of a lifetime.

One of our sons, now a father himself, has a very early memory of not being able to distinguish between the two of us. "Of course," he said, "as a little kid of about three I knew one was called 'Mom' and the other 'Dad,' but it was hard sorting you people out. You both had the same coats. (His memory was absolutely correct.) You both had short hair. (That was also true. When I first cut off my long hair, the sight of me reduced him to tears. I was unrecognizable.)

"In my mind, I thought you could be exchanged—one was as good as another." On occasion, he would jokingly call us "Jois" (Joel-Lois), a reminder of that early confusion.

Before we had children, each of us had established what we thought were pretty clear identities. Joel was a professor of psychology. "Inside" he was feeling quite pleased with himself, having achieved certain goals, all part of his dream. It's not that he went around announcing his accomplishments and career—nothing like that. It was just a good feeling, a kind of personal glow he experienced in his daily life.

He vividly recalls one soccer game. Before the game, one of the new coaches, trying to link children with parents, asked the children who some of the adults were. When he came to Joel, our seven-year-old piped up, "Oh, he's just my dad." Without conscious awareness, our son had identified the central core of Joel's identity at that moment. Being a little boy's dad was a very special role for Joel, but it was a very different identity than Professor of Psychology.

The first real understanding of who I had become, not only for the outside world, but also in my own eyes, occurred a year after our first child was born. It had taken me a long time to finish my doctorate since there were a couple of breaks in my study as we moved around. Finally, I was sitting in a paneled room, facing an awesome committee taking my oral examination. The exam, a mixture of tension and elation, finally finished at 4 p.m. For a scant fifteen minutes after, I basked in the identity of a "happy new graduate."

Unfortunately, I could not hang around very long for any festivities or the opportunity to revel in my new persona. The reason was not very profound. At the time we were living in a university building where laundry times were assigned and strictly monitored. If you didn't do laundry at a specified hour, you had to wait a whole week for your next turn. I had fifteen minutes to rush back to the apartment, scoop up the laundry (mostly diapers), collect my one-year-old son, pay the baby-sitter for the five hours of work, and race down to the basement to do laundry. I was back in my other very real role of laundress and Mom.

The need to switch suddenly from one identity to another was sobering. You will undoubtedly face a whole string of identities in the years after the romantic candlelight suppers of a honeymoon. Recognizing and accepting that reality can smooth the way for each new identity and can go a long way toward preventing any one change from causing a destructive crisis.

If we were unhappy at our families' first hints that our fun and games goal for married life needed some modification, it was nothing compared to our dismay when we realized that to some extent they were right. Like every other newlywed couple, we had to shift our focus from where to play tennis or which bike path to explore to the more mundane matters of who will do the dishes or the laundry, who will pay the electric bill, or whose job it is to fill the car with gas.

For many people of our generation there were well-established roles of husband and wife in our society, roles which, in a sense, no matter how irritating and unpleasant, made the marital identity chore a lot easier. World War II altered some of the conventional stereotypes regarding women working; but, after the war, in the late 40s and 50s it was back to the old conventional roles of husband and wife. By and large, this meant the wife stayed home to mind the kids and the house, and the husband went to work to support them. However, this was not true for our family.

In the early sixties, we were living in a suburban home and vividly recall one son, about eight years old at the time, standing sad-faced in the playroom.

"What happened?"

"Jimmy. . . ." He hesitated, collecting his thoughts.

"What did Jimmy do?"

"He didn't do anything."

"I don't believe you. Something has made you unhappy." Parents are expert at reading expressions of their children and subjecting them to grilling question and answer sessions. We certainly were no exceptions.

"He says everybody in the neighborhood feels sorry for us 'cause my mom has to work. My dad can't *support* the family."

I listened with open-mouthed astonishment. How could I explain or defend my teaching research position and salary to an eight-year-old?

The many changes in American society over the past years have shaken up those roles. Couples today have greater freedom to define themselves and to escape being locked into traditional roles. However, this increased freedom may also entail greater confusion and tension.

In an effort to go against the traditional stereotypes, in the first wave of change, women, men, and children suffered. This is one man's description of what happened in his marriage.

"It's true, I thought she would stay at home like my own mother. I expected her to put dinner on the table. I expected her to stay home with the kids. It wasn't anything like my laying down laws. I just assumed that's the way it would be. At first, we both worked. After we had our first child, I thought she would stay home. She reacted. It was the first wave of feminism.

"She was the first one on our street to walk out. There was a note on the door, 'It's all yours.' No discussion, no hint, no argument. She just left. She wasn't the only one. It was crazy those years. Her friends were walking out. They supported each other's leaving. I guess this was to be expected. At the start of any revolution everything goes overboard.

"We never got together again. My kids to this day do not speak to her. They never forgave her. Nor do I really. I guess when some new idea comes a lot of people pay the price— those at the start of the revolution at least."

Couples today have to decide for themselves who will cook, clean house, stay home with the children or make other childcare arrangements. They have to work out solutions if one is offered a promotion in another town which would require the other to give up a well-liked position.

And all of this balancing is done against a backdrop of awareness of what the stereotypical roles used to be. Resisting those roles too furiously or holding on to them too tightly can take a lot of energy and lead to any number of heated disputes.

In the beginning of our marriage, we "fought" to keep our identities, fending off any changes and, most importantly of all, resisting being forced into traditional stereotypes of husband and wife. We were determined that our marriage was not going to follow the pattern of our suburban neighborhood where the women proudly announced they had control over the inside of the house and the husbands took care of the outside.

Because of our attitude anything that resembled a traditional role soon became a matter for a high-level conference. Figuring out how to preserve our own identities and not slip into stereotypes was quite demanding. Joel had once thrown away orange Lifesavers because "naval officers don't carry groceries." I was not going to let that happen again.

It was only after the birth of our first child that we realized the struggle over who does which jobs was much less important than our ability as a couple to make sure all the necessary jobs got done.

Our first son was a beautiful, gorgeous, brilliant infant. I came home from the hospital and a week later had to return in a frantic midnight taxi ride because the doctor had missed a large part of the placenta and I was hemorrhaging.

"You're lucky you're alive," an associate of my doctor told me as I struggled to regain consciousness.

Overnight Joel's life changed. He certainly didn't have time to concern himself about identity issues. There was a newborn infant who needed care, a small four-room apartment in a university building to clean, a full load of classes to teach, research to get started, and a wife who had been told not to get off her stomach for over a month. We had enough hospital expenses without adding more expense by trying to hire help.

Because of the unusual circumstances, his identity as a typical, traditional male was shattered. He didn't have a choice. Someone had to take care of the newborn baby, the home, an ailing wife, class schedules, research, and student conferences. There wasn't even time to take a crash course in infant management. It was to be a trial-and-error learning period and, because of the many pressures, he didn't even have the luxury of being able to *complain* about a loss of masculine identity.

He learned the football hold from a neighbor which helped a lot. For six weeks he carried on completely alone.

"How did you do it?" he was asked, after I was back on my feet and doing my share of the work.

"How could I not do it?" was his puzzled reaction to these kinds of inquiries. Immersed in the middle of the situation, he hardly had time to think about a cup of coffee to stay awake, let alone worrying about masculine identity and how those so-called feminine duties were hurting his macho image.

In retrospect, he looks on it as a remarkable experience, unfortunate only because of the risk to my health. He discovered he wasn't threatened by diapers, bottles, baby baths, or late-night floor walking with a crying infant. He found that it was no big deal to put a baby in a carriage and wheel him off to class. Luckily, our first son took long naps, *especially* during class lectures.

In our case, it took a serious trauma to teach us an important lesson. We discovered that roles could be switched without throwing us into a tailspin. In the long run, we realized, it really doesn't matter that we each have to play different roles at different times in a marriage.

Every couple has to work out their own comfortable roles in the marital relationship. The routine obligations of daily life have to be met. There will be times when one or the other spouse has to take charge, perform stereotypical duties which aren't always much fun and may even be resented. There's just no escape.

Each marriage is unique. Our major insight into the identity problem was that rather than get caught in the mire of trying to preserve some sort of artificial image of an identity, the goal should be to do anything and everything to make the routines of life efficient and smooth. In our case, once we dropped all concern about who did what and when, life seemed to flow much more easily. There was a lot less dissension and wasted energy.

What we have discovered over the many decades is that, at various times and even within the same time period, each of our identities will include some traditional and some nontraditional duties. Rather than let the minutiae of life upset us, or make us behave stubbornly, we found it best just to get on with life, trying to remember to avoid power plays of who does what as a way of hanging on to some aspect of identity or preserving our ego.

Having had our identities turned all around because of a personal crisis we know only too well that spending time on petty details is a terrible waste. The process of dealing with a crisis can be an invaluable learning experience. One finally realizes how inconsequential some concerns are for the *long term* success of a marriage.

One woman who participated in a marriage study told us about the role reversal she had to face after her husband was down-sized from a corporate position.

"I *never* expected nor did I want to go back to work. For me, after I had my three kids, I knew being a full-time mother and homemaker was the only job I wanted. I had been only too happy to stop working and stay home. I thought, since my husband had a terrific income, I would be free to take care of our home and our children.

"The worst nightmare of my marriage happened. My husband lost his job. I can't tell you how fast we went through our savings. Our families couldn't give us any more money or loans. He was too old for a starting position. We knew a second career was his only alternative. This meant he needed time to go back to school for an MBA.

"You could have cut the tension at home with a knife. We were bickering like crazy. Our marriage was on the line. I shocked myself. I knew it was up to me to get a job. I lucked out. There was a professional office that wanted a mature manager. Boy, that was me—mature overnight. My husband went back to school. During the better part of the day he chauffeured the kids, took care of the house, cooked the meals and did the laundry. We posted schedules on a bulletin board. I won't say it was great at first.

"The stupid thing for me was that initially I was embarrassed. Then I said to myself, 'Embarrassed for whom? For what?' My kids can go on taking piano lessons. They have a terrific babysitter. We're all hanging in just fine. My husband's back at work now. I swear I never thought I had it in me, but I still have my job."

Gradually one discovers that one will play many different roles over the course of a lifetime. That's the multifaceted core of everyone—a complex set of identities. As we were working on a chapter for this book, one of our sons, forty years old, himself a father, flew east from California on business which happened to be close to where we now live. We had a wonderful visit. The hour was late, and all of us were exhausted. He had to get up early the next morning for a meeting.

"You're not going to wear those!" I said looking at a wrinkled shirt and trousers he hung up in the closet.

It didn't take much time for the "mother" identity to move into high gear. The ironing board was unfolded, the steam iron turned on, and I was soon busy back in harness as mother and laundress, with a professional life shunted into the background. And Joel, what was he doing the next morning? Getting up early to make his son breakfast before he went out into the world. Just what parents do for their children.

Decades ago, if someone had described our current behavior to us, like calling a forty-four-year-old son to check on his cold, we would have been aghast. In those early years of marriage, we were too busy preserving our individual identity. It has taken a lot of living on our part to acquire this profound insight.

In the long run, what really matters is the *survival* of a marriage and a family. It is not a big deal if one day you put the toothpaste cap back on the tube and the next day the other person does it. Earning identity points just isn't worth the possibility of sacrificing marital happiness.

EGO SUPPORT—A SPOUSE IS NUMBER ONE

Having one's ego cut down to size begins early in life. When we were young, someone spelled more words correctly on a spelling test; someone ran faster in a race; someone shot more baskets or jumped higher. And, now that we're older, there's always someone out there who is prettier, more handsome, has a bigger house, fancier car, more amiable pet dog. Winning in a game of trying to be *number one* in the world in any category is rough. Even the number ones have problems worrying about the fateful day when they, too, will slip into a lower position.

It would be nice to say that we shouldn't even think about or bother with being concerned about competition. However, life does consist of evaluations, whether we like it or not. Before we were married, we each privately assumed we were *number one*. Once married we were forced to face that, if our marital bond was to be strengthened, something more was needed so that each of our identities was enhanced and reinforced in the relationship.

We soon discovered that, above all, we had to stop being concerned about our own self-concept and to focus on the other person as *number one*. Sounds impossible, doesn't it? Not really. All we had to do was to make sure that, *within* the marriage, the other person was always number one.

You may want to suggest that it is unrealistic to pretend someone is number one in the world if that is far from the case. Of course, it is unrealistic. Does that matter? Does everything have to be objectively valid? Regardless of who is really number one in the *outside* world, each of us deserves to be number one in our home.

Whether the home has 5000 square feet or 100 square feet, the feelings in the home about one's spouse should remain the same—he or she is *number one*. Knowing there is somewhere in the world that we are number one gives us a place to relax, to feel safe and secure, to be unthreatened.

Our insight into the importance of perceiving the other as number one began early in our marriage. One memorable event was Joel's first major teaching assignment at Yale University. The story begins somewhat earlier, however. After leaving the Navy, Joel applied to Yale University to finish his bachelor's degree. The name alone was awesome for young midwesterners like ourselves who were not quite sure what the words "Eastern establishment" and "Eastern style" meant.

He was rejected. It was nothing personal, of course. Joel had an excellent record, but still, all in all wasn't it a better idea for him to return to the University of Illinois to complete his undergraduate degree? We got the message, and we "crawled back into our cave" to lick our wounds and carry on.

The safety of "home" is learned very early in life. After a fight in the street, a child will go galloping home, fling open a screen door and be comforted by the feeling of being safe at last. Well, we didn't have a childhood home anymore, just our own reassuring words about how some people, like admissions' officers, were too stupid and blind to recognize real worth.

A number of years later, after Joel completed his doctorate at Columbia University and had several fellowships, Yale invited him to join the faculty as an assistant professor. Ah, what a marvelous twist of fate, we thought. He wasn't acceptable as a post-war student but would be just fine as a professor. We admit to having a delicious feeling of satisfaction.

Since this was his first full-time job as a professor, there was a great deal of concern. If the truth be known, we were both downright nervous. Joel said he couldn't possibly imagine lecturing to a group of students for hours on end, week after week, for an entire semester in a "foreign" environment.

I did assure him I had listened to a lot of his lectures about many subjects, including things that I had done wrong, so I was *very* sure he wouldn't have any problem with the students. Besides, I reminded him, they're all thinking about their grades. What really was on our minds was our image and the image of the school we knew very little about. Of course, we had built up a whole host of stories and fantasies in which we midwesterners stumbled about naively embarrassing ourselves.

As far as I was concerned Joel was sure to be the most brilliant, fascinating, unbelievably convincing lecturer the students had ever heard. "Remember," I reminded him, "I wouldn't settle for anything less in a husband."

I had had a good model for my behavior. Every bit of my early writing that was rejected was, according to Joel, unquestionably some of the finest of its type he had ever read. It was the *rest* of the world that lacked taste, he always assured me.

I was totally and supremely confident about his upcoming "test." Joel appeared more relaxed as the first day of class neared. He had on the "right" sort of tweed jacket. He bought a pipe because pipes went along with his image of what it meant to be a professor. I went down to a fashionable salon and had my hair cut for the after-class celebration. The haircut was "returned" and even the manager of the salon admitted it was ghastly. However, we plugged away at style, image, and calming the initial flutters.

The first ten minutes, Joel confessed, were a little shaky. Luckily, he got absorbed in collecting class cards, sorting papers on the podium, looking very preoccupied. And then, just as I knew it would, all the stomach churning stopped; his voice grew strong and assured, and he was off and running.

This class launched him on a thirty-three-year teaching career. In looking back over other initial hesitations, doubts, and concerns we have had in many aspects of life, we realize that our belief in the *number one* ranking of each other has contributed a great deal to our ability to cope with the world outside.

LOYALTY AND FIDELITY—OLD-FASHIONED WORDS

Over the years various marriage styles have enjoyed shifting popularity. We've been married long enough to have observed some of these different marriage fashions as well as to study their consequences. A number of years ago, for example, in the early stages of feminism, there was a wave of overthrowing conventional marriages. Mothers walked out; wives walked out; husbands walked out. Their stories received wide publicity, and the behavior was contagious.

For a brief time, something called "open marriage" became popular. Among other things, the concept explicitly permitted and implicitly encouraged extramarital affairs. There was nothing really "new" in these varying styles of behavior; British as well as American upper-class couples had long been active participants in unusual marriage and extramarital arrangements. For example, the Bloomsbury group, composed of famous English artists and writers, *depended* on the startling, unconventional marital behavior of their members to draw attention to their various writings and art. What was different this time was the fact that these unconventional arrangements became so widespread among the traditionally conservative middle classes.

We came of age and married when traditionalism in a marriage was still in vogue. Walking out and extramarital liaisons were frowned upon and certainly not made public. However, as we noted, gradually more and more couples began rejecting these traditions, breaking marital patterns. More importantly, no one was concerned in the least about their image or what other people thought.

Perhaps because we were married so very young, we still retained an innocence which involved *loyalty* and *fidelity* toward your spouse. This attitude clearly was derived from the "spouse is number one" belief so ingrained in our thinking. We naively assumed others felt the same way. We weren't so innocent as to be unaware of public figures, Hollywood glamour personalities, for example, who moved in and out of relationships with remarkable ease. What we weren't prepared for was to witness the same kinds of "breaking out" in the academic world which we had childishly assumed was above and beyond all so-called "shenanigans."

However, as incident after incident occurred, we soon felt as if we were strangers in a strange land. There was the big snowstorm when every road around New York was barricaded or blocked. It took Joel seven hours, instead of thirty minutes, to navigate back roads and back areas, and to sit stalled for hours to travel from New York to where we lived in New Jersey. He said he felt like an explorer in the Arctic because he had managed this in our small Volkswagen Beetle that refused to let snow stop its torturous journey.

A few days later, a senior faculty wife unexpectedly asked if she might stop at our home, ostensibly to see our new baby. After we wandered through a few stilted, polite remarks, she started to quiz me about the university and the recent snowstorm.

"Did Joel get home the other evening?"

"Oh yes, it was terrible. After seven hours on the road, he finally got home. How long did it take for your husband to make the trip?" I asked.

"He didn't get home. He called. It was much easier to stay in a hotel." Her voice had a bit of a quiver.

We knew only too well no hotel was involved. The affair between her husband and his secretary was progressing at a rapid rate.

At the time the idea of our being arch-conservatives or holding on to some old-fashioned morality *never* entered our minds. We simply could not see why these people were running around "on the make," sometimes with far less interesting or desirable people than their spouses.

"Oh, you two," was said to us, not without a hint of scorn for our old-fashioned absolute fidelity to each other. We were the ones out-of-step. Others jokingly told us that even we would have a breaking point.

After seventeen years, on our one block in suburbia, we were the only family left intact. At the university, we lost friend after friend in the rampant wave of divorces. Colleagues who had been life-long buddies divorced, and relating to the new wives was not very easy.

Nothing made me feel more my age than double dating with a gray haired colleague my age and the sweet young thing he had in tow in a miniskirt with a baby while we were getting ready to see grandchildren. I swore at one point that I would never have another evening out where I was the old lady (not that I felt old) in company with young women less than half my age brought along by our "old" friends.

We must emphasize that our insight about loyalty and fidelity as the strongest weapons for preserving a marriage in every circumstance and crisis did not start with nor does it have anything to do with "holier than thou" beliefs. We also can't point to morality lessons or biblical commands as guideposts for our thinking. In no way are we dismissing or diminishing the value and importance of these messages. They have eternal meaning. However, in all honesty, what influenced and guided our thinking more were the lessons we learned from direct and personal experience.

Our observations of people we knew, as well as the results of our studies of marital satisfaction and happiness, demonstrated incontrovertibly that infidelity and lack of loyalty invariably leave in their wake heartaches and emotional tragedy. More than anything else, the late-night tearful telephone call from a colleague's wife asking me, since I was at the university on a daily basis, if I knew the student her husband was sleeping with, turned us into conservatives when it came to marital fidelity.

"We were in love since high school," she said. "We have three children. I don't know what I've done wrong. Can you help me? Why did this happen?"

In films, plays, and literature, the extramarital affair is almost always dramatic, passionate, full of great emotions of all sorts. The portrayal of marriage is usually pretty dismal with the wife some drudge or the husband really not worth one's love. It is not surprising that one or the other partner wants to escape. Out there is romance, charm, everything worth having because it is outside the confines of the original marriage.

Again we are not demeaning any of these portrayals. From Tolstoy's *Anna Karenina* to *The Bridges of Madison County* these "extramarital affairs" in the fictional figures' lives are powerful. However, we feel there has to be a wide, impenetrable chasm between art and the reality of ordinary lives.

We have never been able to identify or document an instance where relationships didn't suffer because of infidelity. This does not mean that every extramarital affair has led to a marital separation or divorce, but it has always entailed some trouble and a great deal of pain from which spouses have a hard time recovering. For example, in one of our cases, a woman, divorced over twelve years, still cannot carry on a conversation without some reference to her former husband and his young new wife. She is not alone. And women are not the only victims of betrayal. Men, too, often suffer a long recovery process. Healing from these kinds of incidents is not easy. The pieces of life are never easily picked up and put back together.

Just as traditional weddings are enjoying a resurgence, we wonder if traditional attitudes toward fidelity and loyalty in marriage will also gain strength and have new meaning. There are many good arguments to support loyalty and fidelity, not the least of which is that nothing in the world can match the warmth, security, and "safe" feeling of the home, a feeling that is often lost forever following infidelity.

We recall a discussion we had with one couple. The wife had a prestigious position and the husband enjoyed equally outstanding professional status. At times, he was surrounded by attractive young women who were ready and eager to make a bid for his attention.

His wife asked him why he has never succumbed to the attractions of the women around him as so many of his associates have. His replied, "I never look. I know damn well what is at stake. *Nothing* could tempt me to run the risk of losing my wife and my kids. That is a loss I could never make up."

We would agree. We are absolutely in agreement with the young man who noted, "There's too much to lose." There's nothing really surprising in our encouraging you to remain absolutely unswerving in your loyalty and fidelity to that *number one* person in your life—your spouse. And, regardless of whatever may have occurred in the past, the commitment we are suggesting is worth thinking about for your future.

Without conscious planning, our private and professional lives became intertwined. As yet, we haven't been told, as so many people our age are, that we look alike. That's still far from the case. However, what did happen was that we have moved steadily toward a closely knit public and private togetherness.

This was quite unintentional. In the beginning, we each had very different ambitions; however, early in Joel's career there came a time when he needed an assistant. Research funds weren't available. Clearly there was only one alternative—free help in the form of a spouse. A spouse would not ask for a pay raise. The most that might be extorted were extra household jobs for payment. I was an inexpensive, convenient source of labor.

And, just as I was a loyal, conscientious employee without pay, working overtime and on weekends, so did he serve in the same capacity at a point in my career when I was overwhelmed and could not possibly handle the work. I needed his expertise and knowledge to carry me forward.

Gradually, we felt we were in a great position. Others in psychology had to worry about assistants. We took turns as built-in assistants for each other. From the outside, this was a "perfect arrangement." We were built-in tennis partners, built-in companions for bicycle trips, built-in babysitters. The consequences were just a little *too much* togetherness at times. While we added dimensions to each other so that the sum of the two of us was definitely greater than the individual parts, we did begin to chafe a bit.

Virginia Woolf's notion of the need for "a room of one's own," an absolute must for creativity, suddenly had personal meaning. We had to get away, to have a little corner we could call our own, somewhere that would not be invaded by the other person, a place that would be our refuge, our space.

The room, in reality, took on different forms. At one period, it was just a desk in a bedroom with a folding screen. At another time, it was the elimination of the dining room to create a study for Joel where he could put on earphones, play music as loudly as he desired, and turn to his desk to write out the great thoughts in his head. Another time it was an enclosure in the basement, a crude sort of partition which afforded psychological privacy. The sound of Ping-Pong balls on the other side just had to be ignored.

Being able to retreat into a space of one's own, no matter how small and insignificant, is one of the important rights of marriage. Recognizing the need for physical and psychological escape can work wonders, and not only when tempers flare in the middle of a crisis. Everyone needs time out to renew their dreams and hopes and to restore their perspective. Those dreams may be shared later, but they must be dreamt first in solitude.

MUTUAL DEPENDENCE

Without a doubt the biggest test we have had to face in all these identity issues has been the crisis of realizing we are dependent on each other. Being dependent doesn't sit well in the minds of highly individualistic, fiercely independent people like ourselves. And, we have no illusions that we are anything special. We strongly suspect you feel much the same way.

It was a matter of wanting to be our own persons. We don't want to be dependent. In the past, many women didn't think critically about this issue. It was accepted that they would be dependent on their husbands in most aspects of their lives. Husbands earned money and supported their wives. The fact that, by and large, women didn't have their own incomes was a major factor for fostering a one-way dependency.

All this has changed with the rise of feminism. Women can and do support themselves. Women can and do stand on their own two feet. From the beginning we have held fast to the premise that we all need someone and want someone to enhance our lives. None of us, as we said very early in the book, really want to live alone. We have a need for another person to share our dreams, fantasies, and daily lives.

However, sharing is not quite the same as the need to balance our own individuality and identity in order to accept strong, mutual interdependence. This insight was not easy for us to learn nor to accept. If anything we actively rebelled against the idea that we were dependent on each other. "I could walk out tomorrow, and be just the same," were the fighting words we said to each other.

Now, we realize this is impossible. It took a lot of living to finally come to grips with the indisputable reality that we are interdependent. Couples beginning a marriage have been astounded when we told them that after more than five decades we *still* carry on about our individuality and independence.

Thus, our final insight in this chapter on identity is that individuality and independence need not be at war with mutual dependency. They can coexist. In fact, they not only nurture each other but make possible a marriage not just for a day, or a year, but for a lifetime, a goal we truly believe you will agree is worth having.

6 Falling out of Sync

We needed a new car—well, really a second car. One son was ready to take his driver's test. The future was clear. If we didn't get another vehicle, we would soon be dependent on bicycles for commuting to New York City, and that idea lacked appeal.

At this stage of our lives, what we needed, of course, was a sensible, all-purpose automobile, perhaps a station wagon that would have room for groceries, skis during the ski season, tennis gear, soccer equipment, running shoes, and all the other paraphernalia teenage boys require.

Our other top priority was color. Light-colored cars show dirt and require frequent trips to the car wash since teenage and preteen sons *always* seem to have homework at such critical times. Our criteria were specific: a dark-colored, substantial machine that could hold icy roads in winter, have lots of room, and be in a middle price range.

We ran from dealer to dealer explaining our needs. No one could have been more "middle América" in their requirements, and we felt very mature and sensible as we discussed various options with car salesmen.

There was only one problem. Joel was in his early forties. As we looked at cars, he became more and more depressed. We finally agreed on one car as fitting our needs. The moment before Joel was about to sign the contract, he turned to me. Shoulders sagging, he whispered, "I can't do it."

"Why not?" I was completely confused. We had spent hours running around getting price quotes, taking rides in roomy, comfortable, affordable cars. I told him, "This is crazy. The car is terrific. It's practical. We won't be killing ourselves financially. We can handle the monthly payments." The neighbors had wood paneled station wagons. We weren't going that far. His hesitancy seemed irrational.

"This car is you, 100% you," said the salesman in a last valiant attempt at a convincing sales pitch. "Look at it." He started going over the features one by one.

Joel turned to look. The car was parked at the side of the lot, a steady, solid, stable, mature, spiritless, conventional vehicle. If it had had a voice, it probably would have shouted, "I've caught you, Joel. You're finally an adult. Face it, you're no longer a teenager. Settled down, aren't you? There's no going back now, is there? I have four solid wheels, a great engine that you didn't even bother to look at, a nice dark green paint job so no one will see the dirt or mud. There's no doubt about it, Joel. I'm the car for you."

Joel took the contract, telling the man he needed some time to think about his decision.

"Don't wait too long," said the salesman. "A car like this is *standard*. If you come tomorrow, chances are it will be gone. Call me tonight. I'll be here until eleven. We can service it for you tomorrow if—"

We didn't wait for the sentence to finish. Outside Joel took the contract and ripped it into pieces. "Call me tonight," he said, mimicking the man's voice. "Like hell I will!"

We drove to a dealership in another town that Joel, unknown to me, had been checking out for several weeks.

In the front of the parking lot was a low-slung, white sports car with a tremendously long hood. The car had a black canvas convertible top over two bright red leather seats—a Datsun 2000.

It was a bit of a squeeze to get into the seats. The car made huge, growling, noisy sounds. It seemed as if the gears crunched whenever Joel shifted.

"Who drives these kinds of cars," I asked, looking at the minuscule jump seat in back which might hold a small handbag or perhaps a take-out pizza.

"Teenagers and . . . " replied the salesman. He caught himself and shut his mouth.

Only many years later would we be courageous enough to fill in the rest of that sentence ". . . and men in their early forties." The car represented what psychologists have since called midlife crisis, a time when adults begin to question who they are and where they are going, and to see the passing years as a last opportunity to change. Breaking out of routines and changing lifestyles seem like the most important things to do—the last chance for youth.

I remember standing there thinking of two big kids squashed in the jump seat with the groceries or the ski equipment. We were still in the nest-building stage of life.

While Joel wrote out a check, I sat in a stupor wondering at the rash decision we had made to buy something so inappropriate for our family. Where could we go in this car? Had Joel completely forgotten who we were and why we needed a second car in the first place?

Although nothing was ever put into words, I could see the glow on Joel's face as he slipped behind the wheel, battened down the canvas top, and roared out of the driveway, hand gripping the manual gear shift. Actually, our sons, as well as Joel, had the same beatific expressions on their faces when they either sat in or drove the car.

I was a more reluctant user. In fact, it was sometimes downright embarrassing to be driving the car by myself and have teenagers tailgate, screaming for me to "drag" with them, honking madly until they pulled up alongside and saw me—the driver. Then they raced ahead sheepishly.

It was a very sad day when Joel suggested we sell the Datsun. It was as if his youth were being taken away. By that time I had accepted the car much like one accepts a pet dog that hangs around long after its charms have faded.

"We can keep it," I said. "We own it now."

But Joel had just returned from an orthopedic surgeon. The low-slung car without any shock absorbers, that landed squarely on the ground, refusing to give after every bump in the road, was causing him back problems. Reluctantly we put an advertisement in the paper. There were dozens of phone calls. One after another prospective buyers trouped to our door, mostly with hair down to their shoulders, wide metal belts, tightfitting jeans, and leather vests. Not one was much over twenty years old.

There was no question that we had faced an out-of-sync crisis such as many couples face about some problem or other. All of us accept the fact that children change and develop throughout childhood and adolescence. What is not generally accepted is that adults, too, continue to change and develop throughout their adult life. As a consequence of this fact, couples often experience crises when their patterns of development are out of sync.

In our case the Datsun was just one of a number of experiences we have had that illustrate the sync issue. The first time really occurred when I was about twenty-nine and decided I wanted a baby. Up until that time, and we had been married some ten years, neither of us was child-oriented. This was probably due to the fact that we had spent so many years taking care of other people's children at overnight summer camp. As counselors and directors, we spent several months of many years amusing, playing with, and caring for 100 children. That was more than enough to satisfy my maternal urges, not that I was aware of any. Even the gift of two mean, nasty-spirited, chicken-liver-eating, Siamese cats which we tolerated for at least eight or nine years didn't awaken maternal desires.

However, the biological clock began ticking and that was it. Nine months later we had our first son. When I began to study this phenomena and wrote articles and even a book on the subject, every one of my colleagues, and even the editors of the magazine which first printed the results, expressed their total doubt. They printed the article with apologies and then received a record response thanking me. It has since become a widely accepted theory, I am happy to say. But what difficulties it can cause for couples like ourselves.

When I first announced the desire, Joel was stunned. His life was all arranged. The idea of having a child disrupting our relationship had never occurred to him. Children hadn't figured in his future plans. The concept was hardly enthralling.

The problem of being out-of-sync was a phenomena we began to observe not only in ourselves but in our friends and, later, in more formal studies. We noted what we called the "camel hair coat" syndrome: when the husband comes home with a camel hair coat expecting to live it up a bit and the wife is in jeans facing mounds of laundry. We watched marriages go from crisis to crisis as couples moved from young marrieds into the nest-building stage before the husband was really ready to nest. We saw husbands in their forties who were ready and eager to "kick up their heels and have fun," and wives who were more focused on the responsibilities of raising children.

The chances for being out-of-sync are always hovering in the background of a marriage simply because male and female patterns of development are different. Husband and wives cannot expect they will change, develop, and grow at the same rate and in the same way. It's different with children when, within a certain period of time, they all start to walk, talk, and give up diapers regardless of whether they are male or female.

Life experiences are different for adults and the rates and changes can't be predicted. Many women, for example, who never before thought of themselves as maternal, are stunned by the dramatic change in their feelings when they have children. The same kinds of emotions in males may take a little longer to develop.

It is our belief that the out-of-sync crises can't be dismissed with flippant comments. "He's just reliving his youth" or "She thinks she's still a girl" miss the point. Being out of sync doesn't always mean an attempt to regain lost youth. These crises result whenever spouses have conflicting goals for how they want to live at the moment. Out-of-sync crises can occur at any age, for example, when the retired man is content to rock on the porch and his wife gets a new burst of vigor and runs out to find a new job, or takes up a new, engrossing hobby.

The best advice we can offer is that every couple must accept that change and development are not going to end with the teen years. Throughout life, all of us are going to be changing and developing, and these changes will happen at different rates for each of us. The process, however, is normal and to be expected.

Thus, the man in his forties who suddenly wants to break loose from the daily routine the couple has established is not out to irritate his wife. Instead, he is trying to satisfy his own new-found desires and goals as he enters a new stage in his life. The wife who suddenly gets a new burst of energy in her forties and involves herself in all kinds of new activities that take her away from the home more and more is not necessarily being contrary. She, too, is starting to think of where she is going and who she has become.

The out-of-sync periods in marriages are stressful. Everything seems thrown off balance. The changing spouse is often accused of upsetting the relationship of the spouses and the children. The whole course of life seems shaky. It takes time and patience to live through these periods. Some psychological space is important so that each spouse can try out new and different adaptations. Trial and error may not be easy to live with, but it is the only way to find the solutions and adjustments that have to be made to adapt to the changes that are happening.

We experienced a long, disquieting period when I was fantasizing about living on a ranch, riding horses every day, while Joel wanted us to get a sailboat and go cruising around the world. He dislikes riding intensely, and I could think of nothing worse than being imprisoned on a boat, rocking back and forth, and being constantly wet. It was not an easy time.

Some of the anger you may feel toward your spouse when the two of you are out of sync because he or she is developing in new ways might be tempered by realizing that you will have your turn another time. You may be suffering at the moment, but your spouse will have a turn at feeling out of sync with you when you are developmentally undergoing change. The stress and tension caused by spouses being developmentally out of sync goes both ways.

In my late fifties we were once again owners of one car. The others had disappeared with our college-age sons. We lived in the country. Our schedules were different, and there was a great deal of tension as we tried to manage with one car. I resented the dependency. Joel disliked the curtailing of his freedom. The only viable solution was a second car. Once again we made the rounds of dealers.

"You have to testdrive this great car. It's all-purpose, a real family kind of car. It's fully automatic so you won't have any problems."

"When I grew up, we only had stick shifts," I replied, not without a touch of annoyance.

The saleswoman flicked back her shoulder-length blonde hair, adjusted her miniskirt, and slipped into the seat next to me.

The dashboard was depressing. There was not a single flashing light to mar its sedate, economical set of buttons.

I was getting a stomachache.

"How do you like it?" she said enthusiastically. "It's a great car! The color suits you (it was a nice quiet gray). My mom and grandma hate bright-colored cars. I had my mom buy a car just like this," she added sociably.

Either she stopped chattering, or I was going to crash the vehicle into the nearest tree. We drove around and returned to the office.

"What's wrong?" asked Joel, perceptively looking at my drawn expression.

"Who said anything was wrong?" I snarled.

"Oh, she loved the car," said the saleswoman with visions of a sale dancing in her head, somehow interpreting my lack of comments as a positive reaction.

A tight throat prevented me from speaking.

"You said you wanted your own car," Joel told me. He really wanted me to get this car because he was planning on getting a practical van. After retirement, he wanted to pursue an art career which meant transporting racks and paintings to art shows. We would need a "normal" car for everyday use.

It was my idea to drive to a Honda dealer, one I had scouted out a week or so previously. In the showroom window was a scarlet CRX with black leather seats and a fancy dashboard with all sorts of lights.

The manager and I sat down to discuss the car.

"It has a stick shift," he apologized. "Can you. . . ."

"I grew up with stick shifts." I interrupted, annoyed again.

"Well, there's another problem that concerns me."

"Like?"

"I'm just trying to give you the advice I would give my mother. I would prefer seeing a young man drive this car simply because this particular CRX, for some reason or another, has a super high-powered engine. It's the kind they race in Japan. It came in here by mistake. In other words, the car is over-powered for its size."

"How is that a problem?"

"You could go too fast."

"I won't go too fast," I told him pointblank.

"Still, if you were my mother. . . ."

"I am not your mother. And this is exactly the car I want."

We shook hands. It was a marvelous car. I was able to zoom ahead of annoying drivers as stoplights turned green rather than have them honk at me. I could escape from overpowering trucks whose chief delight was tailgating small cars.

When our sons heard about my new car, they were mildly interested. The day they saw me behind the wheel their eyes glinted. The car was my pet for years until one son took possession.

7 From "Couple" to "Family"

When we began this book about marriage we decided to be totally truthful in describing the personal events in our lives which led to our insights on marital survival. Since we're in-laws now, we're feeling a little sensitive and perhaps a trifle cautious about this section. But our commitment to provide helpful, open, and honest advice cannot waver.

Of course, when we think about it, there is absolutely no reason for concern. We could never fail to have a perfect relationship with our daughters-in-law simply because of what we learned from our own experience. The guiding principle of our behavior is for us to think first of what my mother-in-law would do and then *do exactly the opposite*. To date we have never erred.

Our situation is not uncommon. We had very different parents. Our relationship with my parents developed successfully over the years, undoubtedly because they considered Joel a "prize." It's always easier for in-laws to get along with their child's choice of a spouse if they assume that person to be special from the beginning.

I, on the other hand, was not the first choice of my mother-in-law. Her heart was set on Joel marrying a beautiful teenager, the daughter of close friends, who, according to the information frequently given to me, was not only glamorous but a musician (violin, piano, cello), a figure skater (a hidden ambition of mine), a singer (operatic caliber), a ballet dancer, an astrophysicist, an engineer, and a mathematician, not unlike her handsome father who was wealthy and possessed a similarly amazing array of talents.

Although this young woman did not fulfill the destiny planned for her by both sets of parents, hers and Joel's, she did marry a fantastically wealthy dentist, lived in homes six times the size of anything we ever lived in, and raised two gorgeous daughters who were prodigies in chess, music, archaeology, figure skating, more astrophysics, mathematics, and I think ballet for relaxation.

Neither we, nor our children, could possibly compete with that combination of talents. In all fairness, we must be sympathetic. After all, who would you choose as a daughter-in-law? Joel and I remember my first meeting with one of my mother-in-law's dearest friends; the woman, forgetting our presence, turned to my mother-in-law and said, "Why, Mary, you said she was a monster. She's not such a monster."

The insight we came to, not without some sadness, is that, in life, our children, our parents, and our in-laws may not always fulfill our expectations. We all make up fantasies, but our dreams of a happy family may be quite different from reality. Reciprocal love and compassion may not be felt simply because someone enters your family.

Lots of cultures recognize this and have all sorts of implicit rules for controlling relationships with in-laws. In some cultures, the daughter-in-law must pay strict obeisance to her mother-in-law until it is her turn to control the wife her son eventually chooses. Every interaction is ordered to keep feelings suppressed and the family relationships stable.

American culture does not support these strictly controlled roles, however. Joel and I, therefore, were free to make our own decisions about how to handle our relationship. We chose simply to cut off anything other than the most formal of contact. There were no angry words, no knock-down, drag-out fights with bitter exchanges. These would have been too painful and might have done more harm than good.

It is not a question of right or wrong. Families will differ. In-laws are not going to be the same. How you choose to handle your contact has to be your own decision. Pretenses of one sort or another may not suit your personality just as they did not suit ours. For us, a *limited*, always polite, relationship was the answer.

Ultimately, we have realized that couples have to recognize that they cannot control their parents' or their in-laws' reactions to their marriage. If the reaction is positive, celebrate and count it a blessing. If it is not, as upsetting as that may be, let it go. Determine with your spouse how much contact can be comfortably maintained and don't try to do more.

The truth we found is that, just as we could not automatically love everyone who was bound to us by "blood," so we could not expect to be loved by every one of our relatives all the time.

We can be number one for each other, but we cannot be number one for everyone in our extended family. We finally accepted that fact. If this is your story, don't feel guilty. We don't. Get on with your own life and marriage. We did.

BABY MAKES THREE

Millions of people for thousands of years have become parents and most have survived the experience. One would think, given all this history and experience of childbirth, becoming a first-time parent would be a "breeze." However, all the information then and now simply cannot describe or really convey what the experience means emotionally, psychologically, and physically for first-time parents.

There are other cultures, perhaps wiser than ours, who handle the trauma quite differently than we do. In Japan, it is not uncommon for a woman to deliver a baby and to return to her childhood home for several months so that caring relatives can provide her and the baby with the attention and help they justifiably deserve.

Even elephants surround themselves with sisters, aunts, and cousins before giving birth so that they are assured of having help. It was more than we could do before our first son was born. We were living too far from our extended families to be able to rely on their support.

The shock was not the seven-pound, fourteen-ounce infant who quickly took over all four rooms of our apartment and our bed with clothing, diapers, changing tables, bassinet, tons of plastic equipment, and toys well beyond the capability of a newborn. Rather, the shock came from our shift of focus from each other to Michael.

For us, nothing that was happening in our own lives could possibly compare with what was happening in Mickey's. Joel's salary increase was not celebrated as evidence of his outstanding performance but as a means of buying still more of that baby paraphernalia. My dissertation, which I had yet to complete, was no longer a profound, earthshakingly brilliant contribution to the world of knowledge. Instead, I preferred to discuss whether Mickey had had a bath and how well he held his head up. Of course, at a mere month old he was already doing wondrous things.

It is an understatement to say that we were lucky in those early months to have remembered we were even married much less to have expressed any concern with the activities of the other.

The crisis of parenting includes not only the stress of childbirth and what it does to a woman's hormones, the awesome responsibility, the lack of sleep, and the disruption of any daily schedule, but also the effects on the marital relationship.

Prior to having children, there were just the two of us, each the major focus of the other. After Mickey, all of this shifted. The third person, the child, became our all-consuming focus. Inevitably there was stress because of the realignment in the patterns of marital interaction.

Then and now there was plenty of literature discussing the emotional issues, the need to make sure the husband and wife give each other attention even going so far as to escape from the baby for an evening out alone. We tried that. The evening was a disaster. We spent the whole time oblivious to the candles on the table and the oyster appetizer. Instead, we discussed the babysitter's competence and Mickey's feeding habits and sudden five-week growth spurt. To have spent money for a babysitter's time and a nice dinner including wine just to discuss Mickey seemed kind of a waste. We decided it would be much wiser to stay at home and have the same discussion and use the money for another piece of plastic to add to his growing collection.

In reconstructing our reactions and behavior with our first child and then our second, we have been able to come up with a profound insight which runs counter to all the advice you may read or hear about. Our advice is to *forget* all this "wise" counsel. It is more important to recognize that for a period of time nothing else counts but the baby. You could be elected President of the United States and your wife would still be wondering if she remembered to cut the baby's fingernails because he/she had scratched his/her face.

Your wife could be looking ravishingly pretty, having shed all the extra pounds, washed her hair, and put on some makeup, but your compliments to her could never match up to your simply noticing that the baby is the most beautiful creature on earth.

Our profound insight is for couples to accept the fact that, for a short time, nothing matters but the baby. Do nothing; think about nothing other than the baby. For a time, forget your own needs; simply accept, and stop complaining about sleepless nights, unnerving days, and endless talk about babies.

What really causes wear and tear on a relationship at this critical time is having to juggle the needs of the three of you. Trying to take care of the baby, become adjusted to parenthood, and see to the happiness of a spouse is just too much. Take one thing at a time.

Just remember there will be a tomorrow; one morning the two of you will wake up and realize there is a spouse in the bed next to you. My, what a surprise, a real joy, to discover that the other person once again exists. No honeymoon could be sweeter. And a comforting thought is the second time around it's a lot easier.

DIFFERENT PARENTING STYLES

The teacher was the kind of person one has nightmares about from one's own childhood. Brutal, hostile, her particular nemesis was an extremely intelligent male—our son. How wonderful it would be to have a short memory sometimes. However, at the moment, over thirty years later, my hands are quivering on the keyboard with anger. Only remarkable restraint prevents me from giving her real name.

Parents of our generation were in awe of schools. We hesitated to interfere. But knowing what was happening in the classroom and unable, after several months, to tolerate the tormenting situation, I took action.

From the start, Joel's approach to child-rearing has differed. He believes it is important for children to confront many kinds of situations. They have to learn that parents won't always be around to jump in with protective actions. If they don't learn this lesson, they may not be able to take misfortunes later in life with the kind of courage and strength they need.

Who was right? Me with my more maternal protective concern or Joel with his "take it on the chin and give it back when you have a chance" attitude? Perhaps one style is more characteristic of women and the other more reflective of a male stance. We hesitate to pigeonhole male-female styles. Let's rather rephrase this and say that parenting styles will differ.

The incident I have described is by far not the only one of our children's childhood and youth. It was definitely not the only time when we blamed each other for either doing too much or too little. There was no doubt in my mind Joel did too much to try to provide tennis instruction in the vain hope that he would be able to develop good tennis partners. Both boys rejected tennis flat out (so much so that at one point new tennis rackets were crashed into fences). I, on the other hand, offered praise when praise was not even warranted. Family feuds erupted over this difference.

Several revelations have become clear over the years. One was that anything not desirable in terms of child-rearing practices was sure to be the other person's fault. What was right clearly depended on whom you asked and when.

Disputes over child-rearing usually involve blame of one sort or another. A child's poor behavior is blamed on one parent who is too lenient or on the other who is too strict. It took us a long time to fully appreciate that we each automatically assumed the other person was always wrong. We discovered just how self-righteous we could be when it came to how to raise our children.

Our insight about how to survive the crisis of differing parental styles has evolved slowly. We finally recognized that there is no single best way of parenting every child. We, for example, were fiercely determined to treat both boys the same. This attitude came from our own childhood experiences: I grew up feeling like a second-class citizen compared to my older brother and Joel grew up feeling indifferent to his.

Thus, we bent over backwards making sure what we did and how we behaved was identical for each child. What we failed to appreciate was the insight we now have: There is no single best way of parenting for every child. The problems and disagreements the two of us experienced with each boy stemmed directly from our ignorance of something obvious to everyone but us—the two boys were different.

Our second insight was something we actually didn't appreciate until this past year when we sat down to write birthday letters to each of our sons. The letters differed as we tried to capture each of their individual personalities. However, the insight was the same. With all the tons of child-rearing research, the books on how to handle tempers, talk to your kid, manage your child, create an overachieving child, work with an underachieving youngster, there was only one thing that made complete sense to us: the bottom line is love and caring.

Thus, while Joel and I continually challenged each other regarding our specific child-rearing practices, we were in total agreement when it came to loving them. In the wisdom of our present age we truly appreciate that nothing else really matters in the long run. What really counts and can truly make a difference is the love and caring we as parents have for our children, each "number one" in our eyes from day one.

What is important, in terms of keeping your marriage happy, is that you each remember that your spouse is motivated by the same love and care for your children that you are. One may love them and be strict while the other, loving them just as much, feels it is better to let them go their own way. It will be much easier for the parents to accept the differences in their child-rearing practices if they always remember that both of them are acting out of love.

8 Ten Ground Rules for a Happy Marriage

Writing this book has been a challenge. Over the many decades of our marriage we have thought a lot about the dynamics of our relationship. We have also investigated other couple's marital successes and failures. However, this is the first time the "bits and pieces" have been systematically organized into a cohesive pattern. Our goal was to come up with some insights we believe might contribute to a long, lasting, loving marriage.

In the preceding chapters we discussed ways of behaving toward a spouse and the insights we gained from our experiences. We'd like to conclude with ten ground rules which bring together and summarize what it has taken us decades to learn.

1. LET FRUSTRATION SERVE AS A SPRINGBOARD
FOR STRENGTHENING YOUR MARRIAGE.

Frustration of one sort or another arises in every marriage. It's impossible to predict the kind and depth of frustration a couple will encounter. Whether it's about sex, children, money, relatives, or careers, there's only one common element—the unpredictability of the frustration.

I sometimes wonder if it would help to have some idea of when we would run up against frustrating situations. Unfortunately, this isn't possible. So, what happens to couples who face frustration? At the height of our frustration, where do we typically place the blame? On the marriage, of course, and on our spouse. What is the first solution that comes to mind? Escape. One or both partners will say or think to themselves, "Surely there must be a more pleasant way to live, a happier way to survive," and the "happier way" they think of is divorce or separation.

This kind of solution isn't necessarily the right one. Obviously, no one wants to be faced with bouts of frustration; however, these frustrating situations do not have to destroy a relationship. They can be an impetus for the couple to try harder, grow closer, and be stronger together.

This idea that frustration can have a positive effect occurred to us years ago and was the basis for a major research study. We weren't studying marriages at the time. The original idea for the study stemmed from some of our own personal life experiences. At the time we were convinced that things could not have been worse. We thought our shattered egos could never be repaired. Much to our surprise, however, instead of being crushed by the setbacks or frustrations, we turned everything around and became even stronger than we were before.

As a result of our personal experience of survival and strength, we decided to look at what happens to individuals who have been frustrated. Our study demonstrated conclusively that frustration does *not* necessarily always have negative effects on behavior or thinking. What makes a difference is not the depth or nature of the frustration but *how* a person responds. We have concluded that individuals *can* turn "bad" into "good." This is not to say that frustration won't be painful, but it can be a learning experience that serves as a springboard to greater effort and achievement.

In a marriage, overcoming frustrations has to be a *team* effort. All of us at one time or another have watched two well-matched teams in competition. One team falls further and further behind. The losing team seems devastated. Suddenly in the last minutes of the game there is a turnaround. The team that was losing forges ahead. Spectators go wild with approval and excitement.

Marriages are a *joint* effort. If the couple rallies together with a clear goal, their marriage has the potential to work despite the frustrations they face. One person can't turn around a faltering relationship. It has to be a team effort. Working together to solve problems and frustrations is an absolute must.

2. LOYALTY AND DEVOTION MUST ALWAYS BE AT THE CORE OF A MARITAL RELATIONSHIP.

All marriages begin in the spirit of loving loyalty and devotion, but sometimes, even without our awareness, we may forget our vow of loyalty and devotion. We forget to try. We forget where our loyalties lie. We become less than devoted to the other person in countless little ways that soon add up to one big problem.

There is only one way to combat this kind of erosion. Couples must keep a high level of interest in, concern for, and dedicated loyalty to their spouses. How and what you do to express those things is a matter of personal style. What really matters is that you never let your spouse forget that you are devoted to them.

3. REMAINING FAITHFUL TO ONE'S SPOUSE
IN EVERY WAY IS ESSENTIAL.

When one thinks about being faithful to a spouse, the first thought that comes to mind is sexual fidelity. Whatever behaviors have gone on before, once married, we are absolutely certain that sexual fidelity must prevail. Extramarital affairs, no matter the duration, inevitably cause sorrow. We have witnessed the pain and sadness that occurs in the wake of infidelity.

However, we are not advocating fidelity just as a way of escaping sadness or pain. Knowing that one can *trust* one's spouse no matter what is a warm, glorious feeling. A marriage in which two people can trust each other in terms of sexual fidelity cannot help but succeed. Our third ground rule is that no matter the temptations, influences, or seductive approaches of others, only one person, your spouse, should be your lovemaking partner. When both spouses know this is an inviolate rule, there is never doubt, insecurity, or tension.

Although we have spent most of our adult lives as psychologists, we are in serious disagreement with the majority of our professional colleagues with regard to sexuality. In fact, we are convinced that the prevailing attitudes and opinions among psychologists have contributed significantly to sexual problems in marriage.

The currently popular view among psychologists stems, at least in part, from Freud (even though most psychologists today would probably not characterize themselves as Freudian), who interpreted sex as a matter of temporary tension reduction that is experienced as pleasure. Thus, the individual, motivated to gain pleasure, sees sexual objects that will reduce erogenous tension and give pleasure.

While this view has been discussed in many different forms, it underlies much of today's psychologists' efforts to study sexuality and to deal with sexual problems. The therapy often focuses on attempts to gain insight into what is blocking the individual's attempts to gain sexual pleasure, and, of course, there has been an enormous amount of time and energy and research devoted to sexual behaviors. It's assumed that if you understand your hang-ups and learn some new, nifty techniques, you'll be able to maximize sexual pleasure and *ipso facto* solve your sexual problems.

But this approach hasn't worked. There is absolutely no evidence that over the years there has been any substantial reduction in sexual problems in marriage. In fact, if anything these kinds of problems appear to be even more pervasive. We are convinced that this is, at least in part, a result of the ego-centric, individualistic, mechanical, amoral, technique-oriented approach to sexuality.

Missing from this approach is the recognition that LOVE is at the core of marital sex and that without love sex becomes a shallow, superficial, very transitory experience of tension reduction that is ultimately frustrating and unfulfilling.

Numerous writers have tried to define love. Countless novels, films, television dramas, short stories, and poems deal with this subject. We do not presume to have a universal, absolute definition that will satisfy everyone. However, we do believe that there is a central dimension of our own experience of marital love that many, if not most, other happily married couples share, that is directly relevant to sexuality. Specifically, this is the spontaneous, intuitive, and profound empathy that we have for each other's emotional experience. This empathy should be at the core of lovemaking.

It is the empathy that we feel with the other person in all aspects of life that is also central in our own view of sexuality. Thus, our suggestion is that you forget about any tension-reduction theories, techniques, or tricks you may have read about in sex manuals or magazines. Focus instead on empathizing with your spouse, experiencing not your own pleasure but the pleasure of the other person. Forgetting yourself and thinking of your spouse will enable you to do what comes naturally, spontaneously, and lovingly. And, as you see, this is linked with the concept of your spouse as "number one"—the central figure in your life for you just as you are the central figure or "number one" for your spouse.

4. ACCENTUATE THE POSITIVE AND SELECTIVELY
IGNORE THE NEGATIVE.

In the pre-marriage dating game individuals are bound to put their best foot forward. People "dress" for dates not only in what they wear but in their ways of behaving. When individuals sometimes say they really didn't know who the other person was until after marriage, they are being truthful.

It's not that people determinedly conceal aspects of their personality or behavior. It's only to be expected that, after marriage, some guards are dropped. People relax. And we must not forget that we are always changing in some ways, so it is not surprising that behaviors a spouse never knew existed can suddenly surface.

It has astonished us, after all these years of marriage, to discover that we are still developing striking new ways of behaving. We call this phenomenon "the bottom of the jelly jar." For many years of our marriage we had always scraped the bottom of a jelly jar. Now, after fifty years of behaving one way, Joel has suddenly begun leaving a teaspoon of preserve in the bottom of the jar. He puts that jar on the table near my plate, and he opens up a nice fresh jar for himself. I am left struggling with a too-short teaspoon, trying to use up the remaining jelly or jam.

You might assume I would revolt, throw the jar in the trash can, and switch to the new jar. This can't work with me because of my dedication not to waste anything.

Now I, in turn, have always saved attractive shopping bags from department stores. Most of the time they are neatly folded. However, now that the closet is overflowing, they are merely squashed and pushed onto an already overcrowded shelf. Unfortunately, this shelf happens to be the same handy place where Joel stores some of his possessions.

There is no question about how irritating these behaviors have become to each of us. Intense fights over minutiae are typical not only of us but of most people. After a great deal of jar squabbling and bag criticism which hasn't really changed the behavior of either of us, we have concluded that we simply have to ignore the less-than-thrilling characteristics of the other person. For the sake of happiness it's far better for me not to think too much about the last spoonful of jelly in the jar and for Joel to ignore a whole shelf of shopping bags that fall out every time he opens the closet door. The goal of couples, including ourselves, should be to make certain we concentrate on the many wonderful characteristics of the other person and selectively overlook any less desirable traits.

A bit of blindness to faults will go a long way toward keeping a marriage happy and joyful. Look beyond the teaspoon of jelly left in the jar and the shopping bags in the closet. Recognize that you are never going to remake your spouse to any great degree. It's a lot easier to accentuate the positive aspects and let the negative recede into the background.

5. DON'T EVER FORGET TO ENJOY LIFE TOGETHER.

We began this book with a chapter about the importance of having fun with your spouse. We believe this ground rule must be ingrained in a couple's minds. It can never be said too often. When we look back over the periods of dissatisfaction in our marriage, we realize that most often our mistake was that we forgot the ground rule of having fun. For example, we were recently asked on a public television show what we, as parents, might have done differently in raising our children. What regrets did we have? What mistakes did we make? We were totally unprepared for the question. However, our immediate and spontaneous answer was that we took them and ourselves much too seriously. We should have let ourselves have more fun with them.

Marriages are about more than merely fulfilling the routines of everyday life. Central to every marriage is enjoying life together.

6. FORGIVE AND FORGET.

There's a high school principal whom I will never forgive. There's a professor whose name is permanently inscribed in Joel's "black book." There's the infamous fifth grade teacher of one of our sons and later on a coach at our sons' school whose behaviors were unconscionable.

Events connected with these people occurred "centuries" ago. However, their names only have to pop into our minds, and we can recall the incidents as if they happened yesterday. Grudge-holding afflicts all of us. The above are only a few in our history. We're fairly certain that you can come up with lengthy lists of your own.

Grudge-holding in a marriage is another story. It simply doesn't belong. Forgiveness is a must. None of us is perfect, despite the fact that at times we may act as though we think we are.

What is critical in a marriage is that, after allowing a short time for the wounds to heal, you move on. You must forgive and forget. Remember our discussion of the invaluable technique called "fast forward"? In your marriage, when the inevitable transgressions, errors, slip-ups, and irritations occur, allow time for healing and then "fast forward." Reserve the grudges in your life for those who deserve this treatment—a fifth grade teacher, a very unpleasant coach. In a marriage "fast forward" is an inviolate rule.

7. A SPOUSE IS A BEST FRIEND.

"Every extra minute I can spare," one woman told us, "I try to spend with my husband, even if it's only a phone conversation. Whatever did we do before cell phones?"

"The last time my wife and I had a whole day together was on our honeymoon," reported a busy executive.

Scheduling time together seems to be one of the toughest things for many couples. In some cases, it—together time—just doesn't work out for weeks on end. When the last time you can remember spending a day with a spouse was on a honeymoon, alert signals should pop into your mind.

Shared experiences have to go far and beyond the bedroom. When couples come together mainly over cell phones on a busy street or every second Wednesday of odd months when both have free time, the relationship may be headed for some bumpy stretches.

The bonds of marriage develop and are strengthened through shared experiences of every sort. Bonding comes with seeing another person, doing things with that other person. You can't just meet over problems or business. Sitting side by side while watching videos won't work. In today's world, couples do not have much reason to worry about spending too much time together. By and large their divergent paths will take care of that. The real concern is making sure your spouse is your best friend, a confidant in as many aspects of your life as possible—someone you see often and not necessarily on a schedule!

8. RESPECT EACH OTHER'S INDIVIDUALITY.

Having just finished a strong statement about the importance of intimacy and shared experiences, now we have to suggest a contradiction—the need to respect a spouse's individuality and private space both physically and psychologically. For us this has been a problem simply because by choice we work together, play sports together, travel together and, in short, spend a lot of time in each other's company. Others have occasionally accused of us of being an impenetrable twosome who have created walls against the world.

We realize that we may seem indistinguishable on occasion, but we don't quite see it that way. Although it may be true that in the outside world we appear together the vast majority of the time, within our own home, we live *very* independent existences. Whole blocks of time are spent in a private psychological and physical world. I have my study. Joel has his own work space. We will meet while we're working, but there are whole blocks of time which are spent totally out of contact.

Thus, intimacy, the notion of a spouse as a best friend, and the importance of togetherness we talked about before, has a codicil. While it is true that we are strong proponents of togetherness and shared experiences, we feel couples must make certain that each has time and space for private thoughts, dreams, and aspirations.

9. RECOGNIZE MUTUAL INTERDEPENDENCE.

It has not always been easy for us to admit and accept that we are mutually dependent on each other. It's something we have only learned to appreciate as the years have passed. We would not find standing alone all that easy. We are mutually dependent on each other. And now that we have recognized and learned to live comfortably with this fact, we realize that it is a very important aspect of a marital relationship.

While it is true that couples should allow each other psychological and physical space, it is also true that recognizing the importance of being mutually interdependent will be an important step toward binding each of you to the other.

10. SHARED SPIRITUALITY UNDERSCORES EVERYTHING THAT HAS GONE BEFORE AND MAKES SENSE OF OUR LIVES TOGETHER.

Over the years of our marriage we have lived through periods of tremendous stress as well as enormous joy. We have experienced the mystery of death. We have marveled at the transforming miracle of birth with our children and our grandchildren. And, as a result, we have become deeply, profoundly aware of the undeniable fact that our lives have involved infinitely more than the material, physical events that have occurred. Arising from these experiences, we have been blessed with a gift of faith, a shared spirituality that has provided not only the inner strength to face the stresses of our lives, but also a profound sense of the meaningfulness of life that is as real to us as any material object.

It is perhaps easy for some to discount the significance of spirituality as having much of an impact on thinking and behavior in everyday life. The world today is concrete, technology-driven, and spirituality doesn't always seem to have a rightful place. But it is precisely because of this emphasis on materialism that shared spirituality in marriage is so crucial.

ONE LAST THOUGHT

Marriage ceremonies often include beautifully worded vows which emphasize love, honoring, cherishing, and respecting one another in rather broad, philosophical terms. We wonder if it isn't time for a change. In addition to the traditional promises and vows, why not add our down-to-earth ground rules?

A marriage ceremony is a peak and public moment in a couple's life. Reciting the ten ground rules before friends and family would certainly engrave the ideas in a couple's hearts and minds. And, for those already married, incorporating these ground rules into your daily life will insure the future success of your relationship.

9 Self-Study Guide

No marriage escapes the difficult times. Troubles, problems, and crises are inevitable. They *can* be survived and their resolution can be the basis for strengthening your marriage. In the beginning we stumbled through the difficult periods in our marriage. We struggled with our stresses, determined not to let our marriage falter, an easy cop-out in our opinion. We did this by trying to stand back every once in a while to study ourselves and to learn from our many trial and error periods. The insights we've provided in this book stem directly from our own personal experience and, of course, are further supported by the many different studies that were part of our careers as researchers and psychologists.

We strongly feel that it was this process of self-examination and self-criticism that was an all-important part of our having a lasting relationship as a married couple. We sincerely believe it would be helpful to you to start looking at your marital relationship to accomplish the same goals that we have.

The following is a guide for self-study. Please remember these are *not* tests. There are *no right or wrong answers*. The only thing that is really important is for you and your spouse to give open and honest responses which can then serve as a basis for thinking and talking constructively about your marriage.

Have fun with these tasks. They are meant to be games with a purpose!

Shared Fun and Enjoyment

This first section provides a way of thinking about a variety of activities you and your spouse might enjoy doing together. First, prepare *two* answer sheets, one for you and one for your spouse. On each answer sheet write a column of numbers from 1 to 20, leaving a space after each number for your answer. Use the following scale to make your ratings:

1. I'd like to do this **much more often** than we do.
2. I'd like to do this **more often** than we do.
3. I'd like to do this **just about as often** as we do.
4. I'd like to do this **less often** than we do.
5. I'd like to do this **much less often** than we do.

Thus, if you'd like to engage in a particular activity *much more often* than you do, you'd give that item a rating of 1. If you'd like to engage in a particular activity *less often* than you do, you'd give a rating of 4, and so on.

Read through the list of activities below, and on your own answer sheet indicate your rating for each activity. Each spouse should do this independently of the other. Don't share your answers until you have both finished.

Shared Fun and Enjoyment Assessment

1. Play games of any sort, e.g., cards, Monopoly, poker.
2. Enjoy some sport together, e.g., bicycling, tennis, or Ping-Pong.
3. Have a date for the movies, theater, concert, or opera.
4. Go out to lunch or dinner—just the two of you.
5. Go for a walk, a picnic, a casual afternoon, just hanging out together.
6. Play with the kids—not just one parent but as a family.
7. Watch TV together.
8. Take a trip—just the two of you, whether it is a weekend outing or longer.
9. Go on a vacation together.
10. Go out socially with friends to dinner, a party, or other activity.
11. Attend some event such as a basketball, football, or baseball game.
12. Exercise together.
13. Go shopping together.
14. Work together in the garden or on a house project.
15. Share a hobby.
16. Help each other prepare a special meal.
17. Spend an afternoon at the beach.
18. Visit museums or other places of interest.
19. Go for a drive—no specific destination—just for the chance to talk and be together.
20. Have a long private chat on the phone during the day.

Write down any other activities that you enjoy and add the numbers to your answer sheet.

Assessing Your Shared Fun and Enjoyment

Prepare a joint answer sheet following this model.
Joint Answer Sheet

Item	Wife's Rating	Husband's Rating	Difference
1.			
2.			
3.			
4.			
5.			
6.			
7.			
8.			
9.			
10.			
11.			
12.			
13.			
14.			
15.			
16.			
17.			
18.			
19.			
20.			

(If you added any items jot down the numbers.)

You have listed your ratings and your spouse's rating. Simply subtract one from the other to obtain the difference in ratings.

First look at the items on which you and your spouse pretty much agree, that is, items for which the differences are 0 or 1. Which activities would you both like to do more of? Take some time with your spouse to think about how you might fit those activities into your schedule.

Now look at the items on which you and your spouse show some disagreements—items for which the difference in ratings is 3 or more. Does one want to engage in the activity more often or much less often and the other feels that you engage in the activity at about the right frequency?

The results provide a basis for the two of you to think together about the fun and enjoyment you might share. It gives you a chance to talk about both your agreements and your disagreements, about those things you'd like to do more often and those things you'd like to do less often.

Ranking Your "Family Values"

This is an exercise to help you and your spouse determine which aspects of your relationship are most important to each of you. First, write down the numbers from 1-91. Read each pair of phrases. Although both may be important to you, say to yourself, "Which do I need *more*?" Do the best you can to make a decision. Remember while you are doing this exercise don't share ideas or answers. Wait until you're finished for the comparison. Be sure to put A or B after each number on your answer sheet.

Column A
1. Financial security
2. Sexual satisfaction
3. Religious or spiritual relationship
4. Willingness to share responsibilities
5. Raising children
6. Having fun together
7. Companionship
8. Physical appearance
9. Mutual respect
10. Financial security
11. Religious or spiritual relationship
12. Fidelity of spouse

13. Mutual respect
14. Religious or spiritual relationship

15. Fidelity of spouse
16. Willingness to share responsibilities
17. Psychological closeness
18. Mutual respect
19. Financial security
20. Companionship
21. Romance
22. Physical appearance
23. Willingness to share responsibilities

Column B
1. Sexual satisfaction
2. Raising children
3. Romance
4. Sexual satisfaction
5. Psychological closeness
6. Sharing same interests
7. Psychological closeness
8. Raising children
9. Romance
10. Companionship
11. Companionship
12. Willingness to share responsibilities

13. Raising children
14. Willingness to share responsibilities

15. Mutual respect
16. Physical appearance
17. Having fun together
18. Financial security
19. Psychological closeness
20. Social status
21. Psychological closeness
22. Having fun together
23. Companionship

24. Social status

25. Physical appearance
26. Companionship
27. Mutual respect
28. Romance
29. Sharing same interests

30. Financial security
31. Physical appearance
32. Raising children
33. Physical appearance
34. Sexual satisfaction
35. Willingness to share responsibilities
36. Sexual satisfaction
37. Fidelity of spouse

38. Mutual respect
39. Willingness to share responsibilities
40. Financial security
41. Companionship
42. Sharing same interests
43. Having fun together
44. Willingness to share responsibilities
45. Having fun together

46. Mutual respect
47. Sharing same interests
48. Physical appearance
49. Fidelity of spouse
50. Romance
51. Willingness to share responsibilities
52. Raising children

53. Physical appearance
54. Companionship
55. Psychological closeness

56. Social status

24. Religious or spiritual relationship

25. Fidelity of spouse
26. Fidelity of spouse
27. Sharing same interests
28. Raising children
29. Religious or spiritual relationship

30. Sharing same interests
31. Sexual satisfaction
32. Financial security
33. Social status
34. Sharing same interests
35. Romance
36. Social status
37. Religious or spiritual relationship

38. Physical appearance
39. Sharing same interests
40. Social status
41. Romance
42. Psychological closeness
43. Raising children
44. Social status
45. Religious or spiritual relationship

46. Companionship
47. Raising children
48. Financial security
49. Sexual satisfaction
50. Sharing same interests
51. Mutual respect
52. Willingness to share responsibilities

53. Sharing same interests
54. Sexual satisfaction
55. Willingness to share responsibilities

56. Fidelity of spouse

57. Romance
58. Having fun together
59. Sharing same interests
60. Raising children

61. Religious or spiritual relationship
62. Psychological closeness

63. Having fun together

64. Physical appearance
65. Fidelity of spouse
66. Having fun together
67. Having fun together
68. Financial security
69. Romance
70. Companionship
71. Raising children
72. Social status
73. Physical appearance
74. Psychological closeness
75. Sexual satisfaction
76. Psychological closeness
77. Companionship
78. Willingness to share responsibilities
79. Sexual satisfaction
80. Having fun together
81. Religious or spiritual relationship
82. Sexual satisfaction
83. Having fun together
84. Fidelity of spouse
85. Sharing same interests
86. Physical appearance

87. Raising children
88. Having fun together
89. Social status
90. Mutual respect
91. Religious or spiritual relationship

57. Social status
58. Financial security
59. Social status
60. Religious or spiritual relationship
61. Sexual satisfaction
62. Religious or spiritual relationship
63. Willingness to share responsibilities
64. Romance
65. Psychological closeness
66. Mutual respect
67. Sexual satisfaction
68. Romance
69. Fidelity of spouse
70. Having fun together
71. Companionship
72. Psychological closeness
73. Companionship
74. Mutual respect
75. Romance
76. Physical appearance
77. Sharing same interests
78. Financial security
79. Psychological closeness
80. Romance
81. Mutual respect
82. Mutual respect
83. Fidelity of spouse
84. Financial security
85. Fidelity of spouse
86. Religious or spiritual relationship
87. Fidelity of spouse
88. Social status
89. Raising children
90. Social status
91. Financial security

Thinking About the Results

There are 14 different values involved in the choice you and your spouse just made. Now your task is to count the number of times you and your spouse chose each value.

Using the form below, go through the 91 choices each of you has made, and tally the number of times each value was chosen.

Summary of Choices

Value	Tally of Wife's Choices	Total	Tally of Husband's Choices	Total
1. Mutual respect				
2. Fidelity				
3. Financial security				
4. Companionship				
5. Raising children				
6. Sexual satisfaction				
7. Sharing same interests				
8. Having fun together				
9. Romance				
10. Willingness to share responsibilities				
11. Religious or spiritual relationship				
12. Social status				
13. Physical appearance				
14. Psychological closeness				

Scores for each value may range from 0 to 13. The higher the score, the more frequently the item was chosen. This clearly indicates that item is presumably more important to the person who made the choice.

In going over the scores it will be interesting for you to see what values your spouse chose more frequently versus what values interested you more.

Obviously, the degree to which your scores are close is an indicator of the degree you two are in sync. You might give serious thought to those areas where you and your spouse are very far apart. For example, what could you both do to make your lives more in sync?

Emotional Communication

This section deals with the feelings you and your spouse have communicated to each other recently. You'll need an answer sheet with numbers from 1 to 45. Don't forget to leave spaces for an answer after each number.

Now, think of the feelings your spouse has communicated to you during the last couple of weeks. Read through the following pairs of feelings, and try to determine which emotions you have been most aware of recently. Select either A or B. For example, item one lists the following pair: A. Irritation or anger/B. Cheerfulness or happiness. Which one do you think your spouse has communicated to you most often in the last week or two? Even if you're not sure, make your best guess.

Don't forget to do this exercise by yourself. You may be tempted but don't share answers until both of you are finished.

Emotional Communication Exercise

Column A

1. Irritation or anger
2. Cheerfulness or happiness
3. Boredom or apathy
4. Fear or anxiety
5. Excitement or enthusiasm
6. Calmness or confidence
7. Boredom or apathy
8. Irritation or anger
9. Cheerfulness or happiness
10. Fear or anxiety
11. Irritation or anger
12. Calmness or confidence
13. Frustration or dissatisfaction
14. Cheerfulness or happiness
15. Satisfaction or contentment
16. Sadness or depression
17. Boredom or apathy
18. Frustration or dissatisfaction
19. Excitement or enthusiasm
20. Frustration or dissatisfaction
21. Cheerfulness or happiness
22. Excitement or enthusiasm
23. Boredom or apathy
24. Cheerfulness or happiness
25. Satisfaction or contentment
26. Frustration or dissatisfaction
27. Irritation or anger

Column B

1. Cheerfulness or happiness
2. Affection or love
3. Excitement or enthusiasm
4. Calmness or confidence
5. Frustration or dissatisfaction
6. Cheerfulness or happiness
7. Sadness or depression
8. Calmness or confidence
9. Frustration or dissatisfaction
10. Excitement or enthusiasm
11. Satisfaction or contentment
12. Affection or love
13. Satisfaction or contentment
14. Fear or anxiety
15. Calmness or confidence
16. Irritation or anger
17. Satisfaction or contentment
18. Irritation or anger
19. Calmness or confidence
20. Boredom or apathy
21. Boredom or apathy
22. Cheerfulness or happiness
23. Irritation or anger
24. Sadness or depression
25. Excitement or enthusiasm
26. Sadness or depression
27. Affection or love

28. Satisfaction or contentment

29. Fear or anxiety

30. Affection or love

31. Calmness or confidence

32. Sadness or depression

33. Affection or love

34. Sadness or depression

35. Excitement or enthusiasm

36. Calmness or confidence

37. Satisfaction or contentment

38. Fear or anxiety

39. Boredom or apathy

40. Calmness or confidence

41. Sadness or depression

42. Affection or love

43. Fear or anxiety

44. Irritation or anger

45. Frustration or dissatisfaction

28. Cheerfulness or happiness

29. Affection or love

30. Sadness or depression

31. Frustration or dissatisfaction

32. Excitement or enthusiasm

33. Boredom or apathy

34. Satisfaction or contentment

35. Affection or love

36. Boredom or apathy

37. Affection or love

38. Irritation or anger

39. Fear or anxiety

40. Sadness or depression

41. Fear or anxiety

42. Frustration or dissatisfaction

43. Satisfaction or contentment

44. Excitement or enthusiasm

45. Fear or anxiety

Assessing the Results

There are ten categories of emotion included in the choices you've just made. Go through the choices you and your spouse made and count the number of times each of you chose each of the ten categories. Tabulate your results on the form below.

Emotional Communication

Category of emotion	Number of wife's choices	Number of husband's choices
Positive Emotions		
Cheerfulness, Happiness		
Affection, Love		
Calmness, Confidence		
Excitement, Enthusiasm		
Satisfaction, Contentment		
Negative Emotions		
Irritation, Anger		
Fear, Anxiety		
Sadness, Depression		
Boredom, Apathy		
Frustration, Dissatisfaction		

In thinking about these results, remember the responses for each spouse reflect their awareness of different kinds of emotional communication. *There are no right or wrong answers.*

Scores for each category may range from 0, indicating no choices, to 9, indicating that the category was chosen every time it appeared. For each person, you might think about which categories were chosen most often. Which categories were chosen least often?

How do the frequencies for the positive emotions compare to the frequencies for the negative emotions? How do the results for the wife compare to those for the husband? If you feel the frequencies of the negative emotions are too high, what can you do to reduce those frequencies? What can you do to increase the frequencies of communicating positive emotions?

Marital Conflicts

In this section you will have an opportunity to consider your marital conflicts. First, make up an answer sheet for you and your spouse by writing a column of numbers from 1 through 19 with a space for a rating after each number.

Then, read through the list of possible topics of marital conflict and rate the frequency of conflict for each topic. You may want to think of your own lives and add other topics of possible conflict. Add the numbers to your answer sheet. You and your spouse should make these ratings independently. Don't show your ratings to each other until you've finished.

Use the following scale to make your ratings:

1. Rarely or never
2. Occasionally, every once in a while
3. Sometimes
4. Frequently
5. Very frequently

For example, the first item deals with vacations. If you believe you rarely or never conflict with your spouse about vacations, you would put a 1 after the number 1 on your answer sheet. But if you believe you frequently conflict with your spouse about vacations, you would put a rating of 4 for the first item. Continue in this way until you've rated all the items, including those you have added at the end of the list.

Possible Topics of Marital Conflict

Rate the frequency of your marital conflicts about each of the following:

1. Where to take vacations
2. Who will take care of the kids so the other can have some free time
3. Where to have dinner or what to have for dinner
4. In-laws, the relationships with in-laws, how often to see them
5. Child-rearing, e.g., discipline, guidance
6. Shopping—whether to go shopping together for clothing, food, or other items
7. Sex—frequency and styles
8. Choice of friends; problems if one dislikes the other's friend
9. Household chores: who does what and how often
10. Major purchases, e.g., car, house, appliances
11. Personal habits of the other person
12. Participating in extended family parties, social events
13. Taste in home decoration inside or out
14. Clothing and personal grooming of other person
15. Communication; enough attention, e.g., listening
16. General attitude toward other person, e.g., criticism
17. How family finances are handled—expenditures
18. Another man or woman—flirtations or affairs
19. Whether the two of you have enough "alone" time together

Assessing the Frequency of Marital Conflicts

You can summarize the ratings given by each of you by preparing the following form. We have only noted two of the items as an example.

Summary of Ratings of Marital Conflict Frequency

Item	Ratings for Wife	Ratings for Husband
1. Where to take vacations		
2. Who will take care of the kids so the other will have free time		

(Continue numbering for all 19 items and any others you have added to the list.)

Now is the time to look at your two answer sheets together. What are the topics about which there is the highest frequency of conflict? Can you explain to each other why these topics are most frequently the focus of conflict? Do you and your spouse agree about the topics of most frequent conflict? If your results don't agree, what are the topics that show the largest differences? Can you explain to each other why there might be these differences?

Emotional Intensity of Conflicts

Another aspect of marital conflicts is their emotional intensity. That is, you and your spouse may argue frequently about some topic, but the conflicts have very little emotional intensity and thus have very little impact on your marital relationship. On the other hand, you may disagree with your spouse only occasionally about a particular topic, but when you do conflict about it, there is great emotional intensity that might have a significant impact on your relationship.

Once again, make an answer sheet for each of you, listing a column of numbers from 1 through 19 with any other topics you may have added to the list.

Use the following to make your ratings:

1. Very little or no emotional intensity
2. Some emotional intensity
3. A fair amount of emotional intensity
4. Considerable emotional intensity
5. Great emotional intensity

Read through the list of possible topics of marital conflict and for each item you and your spouse should independently rate the emotional intensity of conflicts centering around that topic.

Assessing the Emotional Intensity of Conflicts

You can summarize the ratings given by you and your spouse by entering the ratings on the form you will prepare. Again, in our sample we have only listed items one and two. Your form will include all 19 items plus any additional topics you put on the list.

Summary of Emotional Intensity Ratings

Item	Ratings for Wife	Ratings for Husband
1. Where to take vacations		
2. Who will take care of the kids so the other can have some free time		

Look at the form together. What are the topics about which there are conflicts of the greatest emotional intensity? Can you explain to each other why these areas of conflict are emotionally most intense? Do you and your spouse agree about the topics that are the focus of your most emotionally intense conflicts? If your results don't agree, what are the topics that show the largest differences? Can you explain the differences?

A Final Word

The insights in this book were derived from doing a great deal of self-study. What we have done in this final section is to prepare exercises for you which parallel the processes we have gone through in our thinking these past decades. Have fun with the tasks. Perhaps other ideas for self-study will occur to you. In the course of thinking through these tasks, you will undoubtedly come up with your own insights for a successful marriage. What we have learned is that insights derived from thoughtful self-study can be useful as a basis for a happy, enduring marriage.